UNITED STATES of BREAD

Our Nation's Homebaking Heritage: from Sandwich Loaves to Sourdough

Adrienne Kane

RUNNING PRESS
PHILADELPHIA · LONDON

FOR BRIAN,
THIRD TIME'S A CHARM.

Books published by Running Press are available at special discounts for bulk purchases in the United States by corporations, institutions, and other organizations. For more information, please contact the Special Markets Department at the Perseus Books Group, 2300 Chestnut Street, Suite 200, Philadelphia, PA 19103, or call (800) 810-4145, ext. 5000, or e-mail special.markets@perseusbooks.com.

ISBN 978-0-7624-5006-0
Library of Congress Control Number: 2014941806

E-book ISBN 978-0-7624-5545-4

9   8   7   6   5   4   3   2   1
Digit on the right indicates the number of this printing

Cover and interior design by Frances J. Soo Ping Chow
Edited by Jennifer Kasius
Typography: Alek, Amatic, Avenir, Centaur, and Univers

Running Press Book Publishers
2300 Chestnut Street
Philadelphia, PA 19103-4371

Visit us on the web!
www.offthemenublog.com

CONTENTS

INTRODUCTION

GROWING UP, MY MOM WAS A WEEKEND BAKER—ONE OF THOSE PARTICU-
lar women who would work a busy week outside of the home, but on Saturday morning
she would tie on her apron and the house would be filled with the scents of vanilla,
cinnamon, and chocolate. On certain weekend mornings, Mom would retreat to the
pantry and return with a slim envelope of dried yeast in her hands—and I knew that I
was in for something special. The tempting aromas of bread baking were almost more
than my little heart could bear. From the gentle perfume of the yeast blooming, to the
subtle waft of the warm rise, to the florid aromas of bread in the oven, and the loaves
finally cooling on the kitchen counter—the time seemed to be marked in days rather
than hours. But I knew, after the wait, I would be richly rewarded.

There is nothing like a loaf of fresh, homebaked bread, sliced thickly, and slathered
with butter. And, as I have come to learn, there is really nothing more satisfying than
baking that loaf of bread yourself. Nowadays, even when bakeries are everywhere and
a loaf of bread, bound in a plastic bag, can be bought at any corner market, it is the
experience of the homemade, and the promise of the first slice of still warm-from-the-
oven bread, that beckons us to the kitchen.

But for many, when they fantasize about bread baking at home, they picture themselves surrounded by *baguettes*, *boules*, and *batards*. These are all lovely breads, but none are
particularly *American*. In our attempts to create *artisan* loaves at home (even those that
can be done in 5 minutes a day, or are the no-knead variety), we've somehow managed to

forget the artistry of American bread. While everyone is all too familiar with the image of the young, Parisian boy wearing coarse wool shorts, scampering down the sidewalk, a crispy *baguette* tucked under his arm, we are hard pressed to find a similar image in American culture. Going out to buy a loaf of fresh baked bread at the *boulangerie* is not emblematic for America. But what *is* the American equivalent? The child eating a peanut butter and jelly sandwich on supermarket bread? Surely not. Americans were not always a people of ease and convenience. What *did* we make before mass-produced bread came on the scene?

Before I started research for this book, I had *some* idea of what the tradition of American bread encompassed: Southern biscuits, Parker House rolls, cornbread, and banana bread—these were just a few favorites. But I had a feeling there was more to be baked. And so the digging began—through vintage cookbooks, newspaper clippings, farmer's almanacs, and housekeeping guides. Just as I did with my last cookbook, *United States of Pie*, I learned that there were forgotten traditions to be unearthed.

In the mid-nineteenth century, 100,000 gristmills dotted the American landscape. If a town had water in the form of a river or a stream to power a mill, there might be several gristmills in one town alone. These mills became not only places to purchase flour, but were also meeting places which fostered local relationships and nurtured community. Farmers brought their grains to the mill—wheat, dried corn, barley, or whatever grew plentifully in that region—and it was milled for them. A relationship between farmer and miller was truly reciprocal: The miller kept a portion of the flour to sell in exchange for the farmer's meal to grind. The farmer took the flour home to his wife to make the family's bread. So it turns out we too had our bakers; it was just not a profession or a trade—it was something done (usually by women) at home.

Every region had its specialty breads—both by necessity and ingenuity. Due to the rocky soil and harsh growing conditions in New England, wheat was scarce and hard to grow, but corn was abundant and ground into cornmeal for bread. New Englanders baked sweet Northern Cornbread (page 167) and Whole Wheat Anadama Bread (page 34), made nubby with cornmeal. In the South, the wheat was soft, perfect for milling flour to bake light-as-air, mile-high biscuits and short doughs with flaky layers.

Southerners knew this product had its place, though, and they would often combine grits with their flour in order to bake a more substantial, mealtime loaf. In the Midwest, settlers brought hardy wheat with them from Eastern Europe and found the climate of the Great Plains similar to the harsher climates in the old country. They were able to grow and mill white, whole wheat, and rye flours, making this region truly the nation's "bread basket."

We also have many loaves that transcend regional differences, like the buttery Pullman Loaf (page 60) named after the railcars that crisscrossed the country. Therefore, *types* of bread—rather than regions—organize this book. In it you will find the ubiquitous sandwich loaf, breads made with potato, and those adorned with onion. In the Quickbreads chapter you will find the Southern-style Biscuit (page 144), as well as lesser-known specialties like Vermont Graham Bread (page 152), studded with raisins and sweetened with pure maple syrup. With chapters on rolls and sweet rolls and an entire chapter dedicated to sourdough (don't worry, it will demystify starters for you!), this book fills a valuable space on your kitchen bookshelf. For the baker who is just dipping her toes into the land of yeast bread, there are helpful pages on shaping doughs into loaves, rolls, and rounds, as well as sidebar information that might have the experienced baker trying something new.

When I began to write this book, I thought of the home bakers of yore. Women—mothers or farm-wives—trotting home sacks of flour and setting them down with a cloudy "Pouf!" I also thought of how my mother would tame a mound of ingredients by kneading it into a smooth ball of dough. In America our bread-making history is not about recreating bakery-style bread, it's all about making *home-baked* bread. So get your flour ready, roll up your sleeves, and pick a recipe. There's bread to be baked!

GETTING STARTED

FLOUR, WATER, SOMETIMES YEAST, AND FLAVORING—THESE SIMPLE ingredients will make a loaf of bread. It is the handling of these ingredients, and the care placed on them, that will turn an ordinary loaf into an outstanding achievement. The following pages will give you the information that you need to start baking loaf upon loaf of delicious bread.

FLOUR

It seems that today there are almost as many types of flour as there are loaves in which to bake them. But all wheat is not created equal. There is wheat that is high in gluten—the protein that contributes to elasticity in bread—and wheat that is low-gluten. There is wheat that is finely milled, and some that is coarsely stone-ground. In the United States, different kinds of wheat are grown in different regions. They are planted at different times during the year, with varying growth cycles. But essentially, wheat comes in two varieties—hard and soft.

In the Great Plains and throughout the West, hard wheat is grown in abundance. This wheat is sturdy and malleable. It is often milled into bread flours. Soft wheat is grown in the southern regions of the United States. This wheat contains a lower gluten content than hard wheat. It creates *shorter* baked goods beautifully, meaning a crumblier cookie or a light-as-a-feather cake. Today, in an age of commercial distribution, most all-purpose flours are a blend of hard and soft wheat.

Besides wheat flours there are rye, rice, buckwheat, and barley—numerous varieties—each with their own characteristics. But rather than list all of these varieties, I will focus only on the flours used in this book:

WHITE ALL-PURPOSE FLOUR: This is the king of all flours. Standard in home and professional kitchen alike, it is used for many baked goods. It is white, light, and pure, and it's the most widely available flour in supermarkets. I always use unbleached flour when making breads. With sourdough especially, it is *necessary* to bake with only unbleached flour. I use King Arthur Unbleached All-Purpose Flour for almost all of my bread baking because I find it makes wonderful yeast breads, flatbreads, and quick breads.

WHITE HIGH-GLUTEN OR BREAD FLOUR: This type of flour is milled exclusively from hard wheat. It must have a protein content, or gluten level, of at least 12%. With this higher gluten content, the bread produced from this type of flour is chewier and hardier. Because of the high protein content, this type of flour is able to withstand longer kneadings, either by hand or in a stand mixer. King Arthur Unbleached All-Purpose Flour contains 11.7% protein, which for my uses, is close enough to bread flour.

WHOLE WHEAT FLOUR: Milled from the entire wheat berry, most whole wheat flours found today are fine-grained. Because they contain both the bran and the germ, they are still coarse, creating a dense, crumblier product. Due to the added heft, yeast breads made with whole wheat flour will have a lower rise. When making the dough, they also will also absorb more liquid; your dough may be shaggier at first, but it will dry out and become firmer as the liquid is absorbed. Unlike traditional white flours, whole wheat flour has a shelf-life. If you do not bake regularly with whole wheat flour, it is best stored in the refrigerator or freezer. This type of flour should be odorless. If it has a dusty aroma, it should be discarded. Fresh whole wheat flour should be nutty and sweet.

RYE FLOUR: Grown in the center region of this country and the Great Lakes region, rye can withstand harsh growing conditions. This type of flour has very little gluten protein. For that reason, rye flour is often combined with white flour in order to give bread its characteristic chewiness. The grade of flour—dark, medium, or light—is in reference to bran content. The higher the bran, the darker and coarser the flour. The rye flour used in this book is dark grade; Bob's Red Mill makes a wonderful rye flour that is both sustaining and rich.

GRAHAM FLOUR: This is a type of whole wheat flour popularized in the nineteenth century by the Reverend Sylvester Graham, one of the country's first proponents of healthy eating. It mills the entire wheat berry and then adds the germ and the bran back into the milled flour. In keeping with the tradition of American bread baking, I have included a few recipes that call for graham flour, but if you have trouble finding it, feel free to substitute standard whole wheat flour.

Throughout history, Americans have been resourceful. You will also find the likes of cornmeal, grits, oatmeal, and potatoes, in conjunction with flour, to bake the breads in this book. As you continue to bake, you may develop your own collection of special ingredients to bake with. Find your favorites, and explore the past.

INGREDIENTS

Here is a list of ingredients that I use time and again, as well as how they are used. American bakers have relied on them for centuries in order to churn out family favorites. They are the building blocks of any wholesome bread.

FLOUR: (For a more in-depth look at flours see previous section.) In this book, the flour is unbleached and unsifted. You will also notice that, in many of the yeast breads, the flour is not given in exact measurements. When making bread at home, flour is a variable. The amount may change according to climate, humidity, type of flour, etc. It is more important to watch and feel your dough; making yeast dough is as much about feel as it is about proportions.

SUGAR: This can be used as a flavoring, a food for the yeast, and a decorative component. All sugars are either standard granulated sugar, brown sugar (either light or dark is fine), or finishing sugar, like sanding or turbinado.

HONEY: This is used as a sweetener in some of the loaves and sweet rolls. Using a local honey will make your recipe truly regional.

MOLASSES: This sweetener, made from sugar cane, was more common historically. It is viscous, like honey, and has a rich tone and caramel-like flavor. Use the unsulfured variety; it is less potent but will still give your breads a robust taste.

MILK: Use full fat or whole milk. It gives the bread a richer taste and a more luxurious texture. The fat contained in milk will impede the rise time of yeast doughs, but a slow rise leads to a more highly developed, complex flavor.

UNSALTED BUTTER: Using unsalted butter creates a neutral base. You will, in turn, be able to control how salty the breads are. Salt measurements are exact according to the use of unsalted butter.

EGGS: I use organic large eggs in these recipes. Eggs serve a variety of purposes. In breads, they give structure to loaves and are a tenderizer. Egg yolks act as an additional fat giving the bread richness, while whites can aerate. They also contribute to the sunny color in breads like challah.

SALT: These recipes mostly call for kosher salt, which is ground more coarsely than table salt. I use Morton brand. The crystals are slightly smaller than Diamond brand, thus they compact more in the measuring spoon, bringing a saltier flavor to recipes.

HELPFUL TOOLS

You can bake bread with almost nothing besides the ingredients listed and a pan or two, but there are a few things that will make your life easier and the process more seamless. Here are a few of my suggestions:

DIGITAL SCALE: If there is only one thing from this list that you choose to purchase, it should be this. These scales are becoming more common in American kitchens, and once you have one, you will understand why. For measuring out dry ingredients, especially multiple flours, this is a simple way to get exact proportions. One of my favorite reasons to have a scale is it cuts down on measuring cups to wash during clean-up!

DOUGH SCRAPERS (PLASTIC AND METAL): Dough scrapers can become an extension of your hands. For cleaning out a mixing bowl and getting every last bit of precious batter out, there is nothing more useful than a flexible plastic dough scraper. This inexpensive tool eliminates sticky fingers as well, and can even be used as a mixing spoon when making dough entirely by hand. A metal dough scraper lacks the flexibility of a plastic dough scraper, but the stiff material makes it useful as a knife as well. It can be used to slice portions of dough when making rolls or sweet buns. Metal scrapers are a great clean-up tool, too; nothing scrapes dough off a work surface better.

FLOUR SHAKER: These come in a variety of styles, from fancy and vintage to utilitarian and stainless steel. I keep my shaker constantly full and set it directly on my work surface. During the kneading process, when your hands can get doughy and sticky, it is so nice to have the shaker within arm's reach. For flouring work surfaces, it emits an even dusting of flour—never too much nor too little.

PASTRY BRUSHES: This is an invaluable tool for greasing pans with melted butter or spreading fillings and glazes. I use two: one more narrow, for brushing melted butter into little crevices, like those in bread pans, and one wider, for broadly brushing onto dough. You can buy brushes at a kitchen goods store, or even purchase them at a hardware store. Just make sure you reserve them only for kitchen use!

TEA TOWELS: These lightweight, reusable utility towels are standard in my kitchen. I used them to wipe up spills, as pot holders, or to cover dough when I let it rise. Purchase the lint-free, non-terry-cloth variety.

SPRITZ BOTTLES: Certain recipes call for a fine mist of water to be applied to the dough before baking. Just this little bit of water helps grains and seeds adhere to the dough. The easiest way to do this is by investing in an inexpensive spray bottle.

STRAIGHT-SIDED BREAD PANS: I find straight-sided pans make the most beautiful type of loaves. The sides force a clean, tall rise from your dough. The more unadorned your pan is, the easier it will be to slip a freshly baked loaf onto the cooling rack. If you invest in a sturdy pan, it will last forever, and no recipes in this book ever require more than two pans. In this book, a standard loaf pan refers to an 8 x 4-inch pan, often called a 1-pound loaf pan.

CLASSIC LOAVES

FROM THE STANDARD TO THE SUBLIME, BREAD IS BY NATURE SUSTAINING. It can hold you over until the next meal, or it can be a meal unto itself. Because of the use of yeast, these classic breads take time and care to bake, but you will be richly rewarded. From regional specialties, like the Squaw Bread (page 37) from Southern California, a whole grain bread sweetened with a raisin purée, to bread like Amish Dill Bread (page 58), a hardy, herbaceous bread rich with dairy to sustain even the hungriest of farmers, this is the chapter to get you started reveling in yeast breads—old and new. This section outlines the bread-baking process, tells you how to shape loaves and rounds, and will give helpful hints to make your bread-making endeavors more seamless, thus making your bread-eating experiences more frequent and all the more delectable.

Here's what you "knead" to know:

YEAST

In the 1800s, Americans made their yeast from what now may be perceived as kitchen oddities, such as barley, hops, and potatoes—even grapes! It was a process that didn't always work. These yeasts needed to be kept alive, and baked with often, to remain viable. Later, yeast became a commercial product, making it a much easier task to feed a family fresh, homemade bread on a regular basis. This yeast was often purchased at the market in foil-wrapped, cake form. But even these cakes, which can still be found today, had a rather short shelf-life. Cake yeasts needed to be refrigerated and used within a few weeks. Today, the most common form of commercial yeast available is dry yeast—a trustworthy alternative for the home baker.

There are two main varieties of dry yeast: active dry and instant. Instant yeast is the slightly more potent of the two. It can be mixed in with the dry ingredients of a recipe. Active dry yeast has a slightly slower rise time, and this yeast *needs* to be activated and proofed—in this case hydrated—in a bit of water before using it in a recipe. Both of these yeasts are sold in individual packets at the grocery store. One packet of yeast contains approximately 2¼ teaspoons. (That's why you'll see that amount used so frequently in this book.) The packets will be marked with an expiration date that really should be observed. If you find yourself baking a lot, you can buy yeast in a jar or in a 1-pound brick, but it's best to keep these in the refrigerator. Just be sure to bring the yeast to room temperature before use. For convenience, I keep a small jar in the pantry and refill it with yeast from the refrigerator when necessary. Keep in mind even these large containers have a shelf life; yeast is a living organism, but it won't live forever.

In this book, you will find that I use the term *dry yeast* in ingredient lists. That's because I use instant and active dry yeast interchangeably; the difference in the final product is so minute. I do, however, treat *all* yeast as I would active dry yeast and activate it in a small portion of water and sugar. This is to make sure that I still have a viable batch of yeast. By feeding it with a pinch of sugar, and reconstituting it in warm water, I give the yeast a chance to come alive, bubble, and give off its characteristic aroma. On the off chance that my yeast is dead, it would be wasteful to add all the other ingredients to it. I'd find my bread falling flat—literally. This one added step saves me time, money, and hope. This early activation also benefits the bread-baking process by giving an added jump on proofing.

PROOFING

This term really has two definitions, but both have to do with the process of a rise. Proofing is the first step in baking yeast breads, and it refers to the process of hydrating the yeast (covered above). Proofing can also refer to the rise that you desire from yeast breads. When you leave dough in a warm place to rise, it can be called proofing.

KNEADING

When making bread, a picture comes to my mind of a woman in a faded housedress, standing in front of a kitchen counter, a cloud of flour around her, blowing the loose hair that has fallen from the bun at the nape of her neck out of her face. Her hands are occupied with the rhythmic motion of working a pile of dough from a lump of disparate ingredients into something smooth and supple. This image of the woman kneading *is* bread-making to many people. Some love the touch of the dough—communing with the food that soon they will consume; others see the kneading process as pure grunt work. See it as you will; if you want to make yeast breads, you will have to come into personal contact with a mass of dough at one time or another.

If you are making a loaf of bread entirely by hand, you can never knead your dough too much. Your biceps will become like Popeye's before your dough will ever get too taxed. But with the advent of stand mixers and all of their various attachments, the prospect of kneading a loaf of bread can become enticing rather than daunting to the bread-baking novice. With the dough hook and the powerful hum of the motor, a loaf can be kneaded in minutes. But with ease comes caution. It's now possible to work the dough *too* much at the expense of flavor development in your bread. That's why I advise doing a bit of both.

I believe in modernization with a healthy dash of the homemade, so I usually start the kneading process with the stand mixer, then finish by hand. You want the dough to have structure and for the gluten to develop that stretchiness that will lead to a chewiness in bread. You will also be looking for the dough to remain malleable. An over-kneaded dough can be leaden and stiff. And then there is flavor; a dough that is made entirely in the stand mixer risks coming together too quickly at the expense of flavor. The kneading process is two-fold: it provides structure, and along with proofing, it provides flavor.

My directions will tell you to turn off the mixer from time to time, let the dough rest a moment, and slacken. If you are a novice, touch the dough often. You want the dough to be tacky, but not sticky—meaning you should be able to touch the dough freely without having a large quantity stick to your hands or fingers. Add more flour gradually—about ¼ cup at a time. Watch the dough. It may collect around the dough hook for a moment, and then fall apart, sticking once again to the bowl. This means that more flour is needed to make the dough cohesive.

Now comes the handmade part. When the dough is beginning to come together, it should be smooth and lump-free. Now you can empty it onto a floured work surface. With floured hands, bring the dough together, and start to knead—gently. Kneading by hand can be a long process, but it is *not* a laborious one. In most cases, the dough should remain light; it should not be stiff. All of the kneading motion should be done with the heel of your hand. When kneading, I find it's easiest to think of my hands like paws rather than hands. Curl the fingers inward. You don't want to poke the dough with your fingertips, but rather make a rocking motion with your hands. Gently push down in the center of the dough, slide your hands forward, and fold the edge of the dough inward[1]. Turn the dough a quarter turn and then repeat[2]. The motion is quick and rhythmic. Add more flour to the work surface only if the dough is beginning to stick.

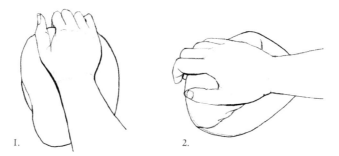

1.

2.

As you knead, the dough will actually begin to do what you want it to do. What was once a pile will soon become a round. You will see and feel this difference in your dough. It will tell you when the process is through, when enough flour has been added. Your work surface will be fairly clean—no errant bits of dough will be sticking around. Your hands should be almost clean—it won't be necessary to thoroughly scrape them free of the dough. The best metaphor that I can give is that a beautifully kneaded round of dough is like a baby's bottom. It should be soft, smooth. When poked, the dough will quickly spring back. It will be elastic. Now is the time to relax (both the dough and your kneading hands!); the dough is ready for the first rise.

PLASTIC WRAP

Call it laziness; call it an economy of space. But I do not like to dirty many bowls when I bake. I use the same mixing bowl to blend my ingredients that I do to proof my bread. I just make sure that the bowl is scraped free of the dough before I proceed. (See Helpful Tools, page 12.)

Many recipes will tell you to lightly grease a bowl, drop in the dough, and turn it over, ensuring a well-greased round. I have found this step unnecessary. The added grease can change the composition of the ingredients. However, as the dough rises, it *is* important to keep it well-covered with plastic wrap. If the dough is not covered adequately, a skin will develop, impeding a smooth second knead. In most cases, I tear off an ample amount of plastic wrap and place the wrap directly on the surface of the dough. I then tuck any parts of the leftover wrap down around the dough to completely cover it. The dough will continue to rise, taking the wrap with it, and the plastic will form enough of a barrier to protect it from forming a skin.

When the dough has fully risen, just pull the plastic wrap from the dough. If enough flour has been added during the kneading process, you will find that the dough sticks very little to the wrap, if at all.

FOLDING AND DE-GASSING

After you have patiently waited for your dough to rise a couple of hours, it's time to fold and de-gas. Most home cooks are tempted to release their personal tension by punching the dough down after its first rise. I used to do this, too; it feels gratifying. But when the dough is punched, your hand unevenly compresses the dough. Small bubbles remain surrounding the handprint, with the possibility of uneven fermentation during the next rise.

So now I fold rather than punch my dough. It's a more measured (and less aggressive) way of releasing the carbon dioxide that has formed during the fermentation and the first rise. Here's how you do it: Empty out the risen dough from the mixing bowl onto a well-floured surface. It will be warm and bubbly, especially on the underside[3]. As the dough relaxes, take one side and bring it to the center, compressing the dough slightly. Repeat this process with the opposite side[4]. Turn the dough a quarter turn, and

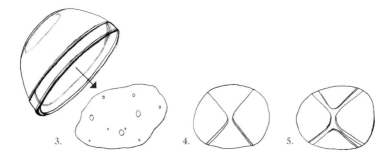

3.   4.   5.

then repeat the folding process on the final two sides[5]. After the folding, the dough should be smooth and fully de-gassed, with relatively few bubbles remaining.

SHAPING A LOAF

At this point, the dough cannot simply be divided and then put into a pan. It must be formed into a loaf, but this should be a loose and quick process.

The purpose of shaping is to give the dough structure for the second rise. I shape my pan loaves one of two ways, and both are completed by hand. When making savory yeast breads, I never use a rolling pin (although it has its place in forming sweet rolls and breads). I find that the rolling pin compresses the dough too much, leading to a slow, uneven rise. The following methods are two separate but equal ways of forming a pan loaf. Give both a try, and discover the rhythm that works best for you.

Method One: Rolling

After the first rise is complete, empty the dough out onto a floured work surface, and de-gas. If necessary, divide it in half, and cover the unused portion with a tea towel. With the palm of your hand, flatten the dough into a roughly 14-inch square[6]. If the dough is too difficult to flatten and seems to be fighting you every step of the way,

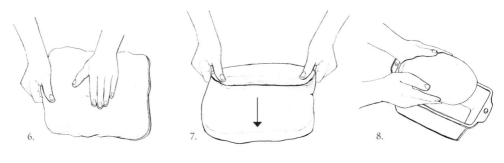

6.   7.   8.

leave it for a moment. The glutens just need to relax. After a few minutes have passed, return to the dough, and you will find it much easier to handle. Take one side of the square and begin to roll the dough into a cylinder[7]. It is fine if the cylinder is somewhat tapered. Tuck both of the ends in, and then gently pinch all of the seams closed. Flip the dough over, seam-side down, and place it in a standard-sized baking pan[8]. Rock the pan gently to settle the bread.

Method Two: Folding

This method is often known as the *head and shoulders* technique. Again, after the first rise, empty the dough out onto a floured work surface, and de-gas (page 19). If necessary, divide it in half, and cover the unused portion with a tea towel. With your palms, flatten and stretch the dough into a rectangle, approximately 16 x 12 inches[9]. On the longer side of the dough, fold the top two corners of the dough down—these are the shoulders[10]. Then take the center, peaked portion of the dough and fold this section down, once again creating a rectangle[11]. Then repeat this process—folding down the shoulders, and then the head of the dough—until finally a loaf shape is formed[12]. Again, tuck both of the ends in, and then gently pinch all of the seams closed. Flip the dough over, seam-side-down, and place it in a standard-sized baking pan. Rock the pan gently to settle the bread.

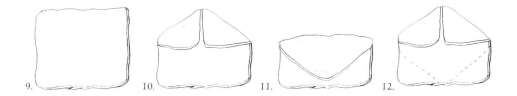

9.   10.   11.   12.

NOTE: It is fine if the loaf still remains tapered after forming or does not completely fill the pan. During the completion of the second rise, you will see a very different loaf of bread. The yeast will have worked its magic, and the bread will only need one final step—to be baked.

SHAPING A ROUND

To shape a round, a dry work surface and friction are necessary, as are quick motions. But before the quick shaping takes place comes the extra step of *preshaping*. This step degasses the dough and readies it to be formed into a round.

After the first rise is complete, empty the dough onto a floured work surface. Gently pat the dough out into a circle, roughly 1 inch thick. Fold one edge towards the center, and then fold the opposite edge[13]. Rotate the dough a quarter turn, and then repeat the folding process with the two remaining sides. You should now have a rounded-off square shape, with a loose handle at the center. Flip the dough over, seam-side down[14]. Now you will have a gentle mound of preshaped dough that is still in need of a general shaping.

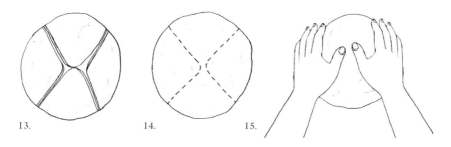

13. 14. 15.

Scrape any excess flour from the work surface, but lightly flour your hands. Place both hands on top of the dough, with both of your pinky fingers planted on the work surface. Depending on the size of your loaf, or the size of hands, your thumbs may overlap slightly. Your hands are simply placed on top of the dough; they should be pressure-free[15]. The hands should create a cage around the dough. Begin to swirl your hands, making a circular shape on the work surface. As you begin to make this motion, the dough will move too, nudging your exterior fingers. Your pinkies will help to form the round[16A-C]. If you find that the dough is beginning to stick too much to your hands, flour your hands again. Do not flour the work surface.

The process of shaping a round loaf is a quick one—try not to overthink it. Your mound of dough will soon become high and round, with a taut skin. The moment you feel a round is formed, cease the motion. A round can be overworked; the skin that has

16A.   16B.   16C.

been created can rupture. If this does happen, leave the dough, let the glutens relax, and then begin the preshaping and shaping process again.

PREHEATING THE OVEN

You will notice that in the instructions, often I have advised preheating the oven for 15 minutes. This is not a randomly prescribed time. Although many ovens today have a built-in preheating mode, I have found that the tone signaling that the oven is preheated is often premature. When baking bread, the heat of the oven is very important. A final burst of proofing happens to the yeast when the dough is slipped into a hot oven. To ensure adequate heat in your ovens at home, I have set the time at 15 minutes. This is usually enough time for most ovens to get sufficiently hot. Also, if you have questions about your oven obtaining the proper temperature, I cannot recommend enough buying an oven thermometer. Set on the center rack, the thermometer will help you to additionally calibrate the oven. If you find that your oven runs hot or cold, make the appropriate adjustments. Each little allowance will help you bake a more ideal loaf of bread.

SLASHING OR SCORING A LOAF

Slashing or scoring are the terms used by bakers for those crusty shapes incised on a round of bread or the gentle crests found in a loaf. Having beautifully scored bread is as much about function as it is about form. When a loaf is set in the oven, the intensity of the heat is so great that it immediately causes expansion. If a loaf has not been perfectly formed—or sometimes even when it has—it will begin to grow out of its intended shape. If you ever have baked a loaf of bread in a pan, only to retrieve it from the oven and notice that the surface has blistered and cracked, this odd formation has occurred because the bread has not been slashed. By slashing a loaf, we hope to give the bread a guide of expansion. We are guessing that the loaf will continue to rise in the oven, and we're giving it room to do so.

There are several methods of slashing, and there are even special tools to do it with. But I think it can be just as simple to make the cuts with a very sharp knife or, better yet, a utility blade that can be purchased at a home improvement store. (Obviously, keep the blades for kitchen use separate from all-purpose utility blades!) When scoring a pan loaf, I recommend one of two methods. The first is supremely simple. Take a blade and make a straight cut, approximately ¼ inch deep, down the center of the loaf[17]. Upon baking, this will create two half-moon shapes, very similar to the shape that is created

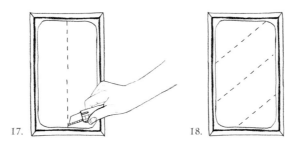

in standard, store-bought loaves of bread. The next method is to make three diagonal slashes, ¼ inch deep and equidistant from each other[18]. This allows for even further expansion and has a more hand-made quality to it.

Although there is no specific look for a round loaf of bread, it is still important to score the loaf. Simply make slashes, ¼ inch deep, along the surface of the round. You can slash in a criss-cross pattern, or a tic-tac-toe board shape, or any pattern that appeals to you. The round will continue to proof in the oven, and the markings will turn into crackly crusts.

As I said before, slashing is a personal preference. If you like an even more rustic look to your breads and do not mind the unexpected protrusions, don't slash your bread. Above all, these methods have to do with aesthetics, not the taste of your bread.

MAKING YEAST BREAD—A TIMELINE

Making yeast bread requires a bit of planning and patience. Here is a brief overview of the process, reviewing all the steps we've covered in this chapter. (But rest assured, all these steps are also detailed in the actual recipes!)

• Proof the yeast, about 10 minutes of inactive time.

• Begin to make the dough by mixing the ingredients with some of the flour.

• Add the proofed yeast to the dough mixture.

• Begin to knead in more flour to make a smooth, elastic dough. This process will take anywhere from 6 to 10 minutes.

• Scrape the dough onto a well-floured work surface.

• Gently knead the dough into a round.

• Put the dough back into the bowl, and cover with plastic wrap right on the surface of the dough.

• Let the dough rise in a warm, draft-free place for 1 to 2 hours, or until doubled in bulk.

• Empty the dough out onto a well-floured work surface.

• De-gas the dough by folding it.

• Separate and form the dough into loaves or rounds. Place the dough into baking pans.

• Cover the dough with plastic wrap or a tea towel.

• Let rise until the dough is just cresting the lip of the bread pan, or has doubled in bulk, 1 to 2 hours.

• Fifteen minutes prior to baking, preheat the oven.

• Slash the loaves.

• If applicable, glaze the loaves and sprinkle them with any toppings.

• Bake for suggested time.

• Remove from the oven; place on a cooling rack for 5 to 10 minutes.

• Remove the loaves from their pans and continue to cool to room temperature.

Basic White Loaf

PEANUT BUTTER AND JELLY SANDWICHES; GRILLED CHEESE; HOT, BUTTERED TOAST—HOW WOULD anyone eat these foods without a much-loved slice of white bread? With its fluffy, pure interior and its chewy crust cresting over the top of the pan, this is the loaf that many think of—or better yet, dream of—at the mention of a home-baked loaf of bread.

In the recent past, this bread has been much maligned for its snowy white insides, and its "hollow" calories, but I will defend it through and through. It is true that white bread, sealed in plastic and tossed in your grocery cart, is neither good for you nor particularly good-tasting. But home-baked white bread is another carbohydrate entirely. This is the bread of our heritage—of school lunches and hot, open-faced turkey sandwiches. It's as good with a smear of salted butter as it is toasted and dusted with cinnamon-sugar. This bread is just downright delicious.

Rich with milk and butter, and lightly sweetened with honey, this bread is also wholesome. Because of the dairy added to the recipe, this bread can take some time to rise, especially when baking in cold climates. But as your grandmother might have told you, "Patience is a virtue." And trust me, it's worth the wait.

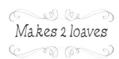

Makes 2 loaves

¼ cup warm water (100° to 115°F)

2¼ teaspoons (1 package) dry yeast

Pinch of sugar

1½ cups whole milk, at room temperature

4 tablespoons (2 ounces) unsalted butter,
at room temperature

3 tablespoons honey

2 teaspoons kosher salt

4½ to 5 cups (1 pound, 6½ ounces
to 1 pound, 9 ounces) all-purpose flour

In a small bowl or glass, mix the water, yeast, and sugar together. Allow the mixture to bloom. It should become bubbly and smell yeasty, about 10 minutes.

In the bowl of a stand mixer fitted with the paddle attachment, add the milk, butter, honey, salt, and 2½ cups (12½ ounces) of flour. At low speed, mix until just combined. Add the yeast mixture, and mix briefly. Add another cup of flour, and continue to mix at low speed, until the mixture becomes web-like and more difficult to mix with the paddle attachment.

Remove the paddle and attach the dough hook. With the mixer on low speed, begin kneading with the dough hook, adding additional flour in ¼- to ½-cup increments. The dough will become a more cohesive mass, more elastic, and start to pull away from the sides of the bowl. It is important to watch the dough during this process. All of the flour should be incorporated at each step, but you don't want the dough to become too dry or heavy. Stop the mixer intermittently and touch the dough; it should still be tacky, but not too sticky. The dough will take anywhere from 2 to 2½ cups (10 to 12½ ounces) of additional flour. It should be smooth and free of lumps. This kneading process will take 6 to 10 minutes.

Empty the dough out onto a well-floured surface, scrape the bowl with a pastry scraper, adding any bits of dough from the bowl to the mound, and gently knead it into a ball. Put it back into the bowl, and place a piece of plastic wrap on the surface of the dough.

Place it in a warm spot, and let it rise 1½ to 2 hours, or until doubled in bulk.

Pull back the plastic wrap, and empty the dough out onto a well-floured surface. Fold the dough over, once in each direction, to release the gases. Divide the dough in half; each half will be a little over 1 pound. Then form it into a loaf either by rolling or folding (pages 20–21). Tuck the ends under, press the seams of dough together, and place in a loaf pan. Repeat the process with the second portion of dough.

Cover the pans with plastic wrap, and let the loaves rise for 1 to 1½ hours, or until doubled in bulk. The loaves should be just cresting the lip of the pan. The bread will continue to rise when baked.

Arrange the oven rack in the middle of the oven, and fifteen minutes prior to baking, preheat to 375°F.

Immediately before baking, remove the plastic wrap and slash the loaves (page 23–24). Place the pans in the center of the oven and bake for approximately 40 minutes, rotating the pans once at the halfway point.

Remove the loaves from the oven, and set them on a cooling rack for approximately 5 minutes. Release the loaves from the pans, and allow them to cool to room temperature before enjoying.

Basic White Loaf
(COMPLETELY BY-HAND METHOD)

MAKING BREAD ENTIRELY BY HAND MADE ME A BETTER, MORE INTUITIVE BAKER. I FIND THAT GETTING your hands dirty and truly feeling the transformation of the ingredients into a smooth, elastic ball of dough helps you to understand the bread-baking process. These instructions are for the Basic White Loaf, but this method can easily be interchanged with all of the yeast doughs in this book. Simply stir the wet ingredients into the dry ingredients, and follow the kneading instructions listed. The process requires some stamina, but you will find that it does not actually take too much longer than the stand mixer method. Give this method a try—at least once—and see if you're a better baker for it!

Makes 2 loaves

In a small bowl or glass, mix the water, yeast, and sugar together. Allow the mixture to bloom. It should become bubbly and smell yeasty, about 10 minutes.

In a large mixing bowl, add the milk, butter, honey, salt, and 2 cups (10 ounces) of flour. With a wooden spoon, stir well, about 50 strokes, until the mixture is free of lumps and the consistency of pancake batter. Add 2 more cups (10 ounces) of flour and the yeast mixture, and continue to mix with the wooden spoon until the dough is well-moistened and begins to form a shaggy ball. Measure out the final cup (5 ounces) of flour, and reserve it in a separate, small bowl.

Flour the work surface well with flour from the small bowl, and empty out the dough. Scrape the mixing bowl with a pastry scraper, flour your hands, and then begin to knead. Soon the dough will coalesce and begin to form a more cohesive mass. If at any time the dough becomes sticky, flour the work surface again with flour from the bowl. The kneading process will take anywhere from 8 to 10 minutes. After about 5 minutes, you will begin to see and feel a difference in the dough. It will begin to smooth out; the kneading process will become easier, and the dough less sticky.

At the end of the kneading, your dough will be elastic and smooth. The dough will have taken at least $\frac{1}{2}$ cup ($2\frac{1}{2}$ ounces) of additional flour. Knead the dough gently into a ball. Put it back into the mixing bowl, and place a piece of plastic wrap on the surface of the dough. Proceed with the rising and forming processes as directed in the previous recipe.

Buttermilk Bread

BUTTERMILK'S NAME MAY BE DECEIVING, BUT ITS FLAVOR CAN'T BE BEAT. ITS MONIKER COMES FROM the creation of whey when you're churning butter—butter milk. The milk solids coagulate and form the butter, while the excess liquid creates buttermilk. So while it is a thick and creamy liquid, it's actually low in fat—all of that richness is saved for making butter!

Buttermilk is an especially delicious ingredient in bread. It has a gentle tang, and the acid helps to tenderize the glutens in the flour, making the bread supremely moist and pillow-soft. When buying buttermilk at the market, you will most likely find two kinds—low-fat and non-fat. When you can, always buy the low-fat version; it's good to have a little extra richness from the additional fat.

To make Buttermilk Bread, simply substitute buttermilk for the whole milk used in the Basic White Loaf, and proceed with the rest of the recipe.

Buttermilk Substitution

Not everyone keeps a quart of buttermilk in the refrigerator, but you still may desire the tanginess that you get from this sort of dairy. In a pinch, you can substitute whole milk mixed with a little distilled or apple cider vinegar for buttermilk. Measure a scant cup of whole milk, and mix in 1 tablespoon of vinegar. Wait a few moments; the milk will thicken considerably and take on a similar tangy taste.

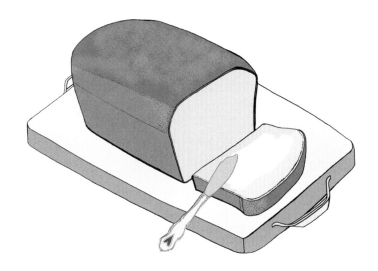

Whole Wheat Bread

SOMETIMES YOU WANT SOMETHING A LITTLE STURDIER AND MORE HEALTHFUL THAN THE BASIC WHITE
Loaf; that's when you turn to whole wheat flour. This flour has the entire berry milled in—both bran and germ—giving it a nuttier flavor and a chewier texture; however, it can be a little dense. That's why, when making a sandwich-style loaf, it's often blended with all-purpose flour.

This recipe creates a whole wheat loaf that is lighter in color but still remarkably flavorful.

Follow the same directions for the Basic White Loaf, but increase the milk to 2 cups. The bran in whole wheat flours absorbs more liquid than all-purpose flour. Substitute 2 cups (10 ounces) of whole wheat flour for cups of all-purpose flour to make the initial batter, and then finish the recipe with all-purpose flour as directed. You should need about 2½ to 3 cups (12½ to 15 ounces) of all-purpose flour in total.

Wild Rice Bread

NATIVE TO THE NEW WORLD, WILD RICE WAS ONE OF THE FIRST GRAINS THAT THE NATIVE AMERICANS used to trade with European settlers. All these years later, this grain still flourishes in the Great Lakes region. But this grain isn't actually a grain at all; wild rice is actually an aquatic grass that necessitates careful harvest in shallow waters. In Minnesota, a state that is one of the world's top producers of wild rice, they eat this "grain" in a variety of different ways—like making this humble bread with it.

I use the Buttermilk Bread for making these loaves, although any one of the standard loaves—the Basic White, or the Whole Wheat—is also superb. Studded with cooked wild rice, this bread is chewy and flavorful. Brushed with a beaten egg, and finally sprinkled with sesame and poppy seed, this loaf makes great sandwiches, wonderful toast, and even a superb savory stuffing (see page 196).

Makes 2 loaves

Buttermilk Bread recipe, using only
4 to 4½ cups all-purpose flour
I cup cooked wild rice (see note)
I tablespoon poppy seeds
I tablespoon sesame seeds
I egg

Follow the Buttermilk Bread recipe, adding the wild rice when you add the yeast mixture. The bread might require less flour during the kneading process, so touch the dough often for tackiness. Continue with the recipe through the first rise.

Pull back the plastic wrap, and empty the dough out onto a well-floured surface. Fold the dough over, once in each direction, to release the gases. Divide the dough in half; each half will be approximately 1½ pounds. Tuck the ends under, press the seams of dough together, and place in a loaf pan. Repeat the process with the second portion of dough.

Cover the pans with plastic wrap, and let the loaves rise for 1 to 1½ hours, or until doubled in bulk. The loaves should be just cresting the lip of the pan. The bread will continue to rise when baked.

Arrange the oven rack in the middle of the oven, and fifteen minutes prior to baking, preheat to 375°F.

Before baking, remove the plastic wrap and slash the loaves (pages 23–24). Mix the poppy and the sesame together. Beat the egg with 1 tablespoon of water, then brush the loaves with the egg wash. Sprinkle on the seeds. Place the pans in the center of the oven, and bake for approximately 40 minutes, rotating the pans once at the halfway point.

Remove the loaves from the oven, and set them on a cooling rack for approximately 5 minutes. Release the loaves from the pans, and allow them to cool to room temperature before enjoying.

NOTE: 1 cup of cooked wild rice is made from ⅓ cup of dry wild rice simmered in 1 cup of salted water for 50 to 60 minutes, or until the liquid is absorbed and the rice is chewy.

Whole Wheat Anadama Bread

THIS HEARTY NEW ENGLAND BREAD IS THE STUFF THAT LEGENDS WERE MADE OF. HERE IS HOW THE story goes: There was a curmudgeonly old fisherman whose wife was a less-than-stellar cook. Night after night, he came home, cold, wet, and tired, and sat down to the only thing his wife Anna knew how to cook: a bowl of cornmeal mush flavored with molasses. He would complain, pounding his fists against the dining table, proclaiming "Not this again." (Today his wife could have remarked, "Quit your complaining, and let's go out for Chinese then!" but this was the early nineteenth century.) Finally he got tired of the mush, added some flour, a cake of yeast, let the whole thing rise, and baked himself a loaf of bread, all the while muttering, "Anna, damn her! Anna, damn her!" When the bread came out of the oven, it was delicious, and a new style of bread was born—the Anadama.

I'm not so sure if I believe the tale, but it *is* entertaining, and it provides a good story to go along with this satisfying loaf. You start this bread by making a cornmeal mush, much like Anna may have done for her dearest. The cornmeal is flavored with molasses, making it dark and fragrant, and then it is combined with the makings of a basic bread dough. I wanted the bread to have a real stick-to-your-ribs quality to it, so I added some whole wheat flour, and that did the trick—it's a stand-out. This makes great breakfast toast, but it is also superb with a cup of New England clam chowder.

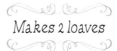

Makes 2 loaves

½ cup (2½ ounces) cornmeal

1 cup whole milk

½ cup molasses

3 tablespoons (1½ ounces) unsalted butter

2 teaspoons kosher salt

¼ cup warm water (100° to 115°F)

2¼ teaspoons (1 package) dry yeast

Pinch of sugar

1½ cups (7½ ounces) whole wheat flour

2½ to 3 cups (12½ to 15 ounces) all-purpose flour

In a medium-size saucepan, whisk the cornmeal, milk, and 1 cup of water, not warmed, together. Over a medium heat, whisking constantly, bring the mixture to a simmer. The cornmeal will absorb the liquid and become more difficult to stir. When the mixture has reached a porridge consistency, about 5 minutes, remove it from the heat. Mix in the molasses, butter, and salt, and cool to room temperature, about 20 minutes.

In a small bowl or glass, mix $1/4$ cup warm water, yeast, and sugar together. Allow the mixture to bloom. It should become bubbly and smell yeasty, about 10 minutes.

In the bowl of a stand mixer fitted with the paddle attachment, add the cornmeal mush mixture and the whole wheat flour. At low speed, mix until just combined. Add the yeast mixture, and mix briefly. Add 1 cup (5 ounces) of all-purpose flour, and continue to mix at low speed, until the mixture becomes web-like and more difficult to mix with the paddle attachment.

Remove the paddle and attach the dough hook. With the mixer on low speed, begin kneading with the dough hook, adding additional flour in $1/4$- to $1/2$-cup increments. The dough will become a more cohesive mass, more elastic, and start to pull away from the sides of the bowl. It is important to watch the dough during this process. All of the flour should be incorporated at each step, but you don't want the dough to become too dry or heavy. Stop the mixer intermittently and touch the dough; it should still be tacky, but not too sticky. The dough will take anywhere from $1/2$ to 2 cups ($7/2$ to 10 ounces) of additional all-purpose flour. It should be smooth and free of lumps. This kneading process will take 6 to 10 minutes.

Empty the dough out onto a well-floured surface, scrape the bowl with a pastry scraper, adding any bits of dough from the bowl to the mound, and gently knead it into a ball. Put it back into the bowl, and place a piece of plastic wrap on the surface of the dough.

Place it in a warm spot, and let it rise $1/2$ to 2 hours, or until doubled in bulk.

Pull back the plastic wrap, and empty the dough onto a well-floured surface. Fold the dough over, once in each direction, to release the gases. Divide the dough in half; each half will be approximately $1/2$ pounds. Then form into a loaf either by rolling or folding (pages 20–21). Tuck the ends under, press the seams together, and place in a loaf pan. Repeat the process with the second portion of dough.

Cover the pans with plastic wrap, and let the loaves rise for 1 to $1/2$ hours, or until doubled in bulk. The loaves should be just cresting the lip of the pan. The bread will continue to rise when baked.

Arrange the oven rack in the middle of the oven, and fifteen minutes prior to baking, preheat to 350°F.

Immediately before baking, remove the plastic wrap and slash the loaves (page 23). Place the pans in the center of the oven and bake for approximately 45 to 50 minutes, rotating the pans once at the halfway point.

Remove the loaves from the oven, and set them on a cooling rack for approximately 5 minutes. Release the loaves from the pans, and allow them to cool to room temperature before enjoying.

YEAST AMOUNTS

As you thumb through the various commercial yeast bread recipes in this book, you'll see that the amount often called for is 2¼ teaspoons of dry yeast with a proofing time of 1 to 2 hours. The 2¼ teaspoons is the amount that is sold in an individual packet of dry yeast, and the time allotted is just right in order to make a flavorful loaf of bread. Can you make a loaf of bread with a varied amount of yeast, varying your proofing times? Sure.

In cookbooks from the mid-twentieth century, loaves often used an abundance of dry yeast, therefore having relatively short proofing times. These recipes were about ease of preparation—and not necessarily baking the most flavorful loaf of bread. It takes time for gluten to develop, flour to become completely hydrated, and ingredients to meld and become delicious.

In most cases, I find that using one packet of dry yeast makes a great loaf of bread. But experiment for yourself. Can dough rise and bread be made using only a quarter teaspoon of yeast? Absolutely—but be prepared to do some waiting for that bread. If you're in a rush, can you add bit more yeast to your dough to make it rise more quickly? Of course—your loaf just may not be as sumptuous and wheaty as a loaf made with less yeast. These nuances are what make baking bread such a delectable experiment!

Squaw Bread

SQUAW BREAD BECAME A SPECIALTY AT BAKERIES AND RESTAURANTS THROUGHOUT SOUTHERN CALI-
fornia in the 1970s for its subtle sweetness and whole grain goodness. Nowadays, it has been replaced with crusty "artisan" loaves, but there is something wonderful about this homey bread. I love the nuttiness of the varying grains of flour and the chewy texture of this bread. And once *you* try this bread, I'm pretty sure that you'll love it too, and will join me in saying— bring Squaw Bread back!

As you look over the ingredients listed, you'll notice raisins, but I wouldn't call this bread a raisin bread. This bread gets some of its sweetness from a purée that is made from raisins, honey, and brown sugar. The purée is deep in tone and sticky; it is rich and reminiscent of molasses. It makes for the perfect sweetener. This recipe makes three good-sized rounds. If this more than your family can eat, once cooled, the loaves easily can be wrapped and frozen.

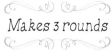

Makes 3 rounds

I cup boiling water

¼ cup honey

¼ cup (1½ ounces) brown sugar, packed

¼ cup (1¼ ounces) raisins

I cup whole milk

¼ cup warm water (100° to 115°F)

4½ teaspoons (2 packages) dry yeast

Pinch of sugar

1½ cups (7½ ounces) rye flour

1½ cups (7½ ounces) whole wheat flour

2 teaspoons kosher salt

3 to 3½ cups (15 ounces to 1 pound, 1½ ounces) all-purpose flour

Cornmeal, for dusting the pans

In the bowl of a food processor or a blender stir the boiling water, honey, brown sugar, and raisins together. Allow the raisins to reconstitute for about 15 minutes, and then process until smooth. Stir in the milk, and set aside.

In a small bowl or glass, mix the warm water, yeast, and sugar together. Allow the mixture to bloom. It should become bubbly and smell yeasty, about 10 minutes.

In the bowl of a stand mixer fitted with the paddle attachment, mix the rye flour, whole wheat flour, and salt together until just combined. Add the raisin mixture, the yeast, and 2 cups (10 ounces) of the all-purpose flour, and at low speed, mix until combined. The mixture will become web-like and be more difficult to mix with the paddle attachment.

Remove the paddle and attach the dough hook. With the mixer on low speed, begin kneading with the dough hook, adding additional all-purpose flour in ¼- to ½-cup increments. The dough will become a more cohesive mass, more elastic, and start to pull away from the sides of the bowl. It is important to watch the dough during this process. All of the flour should be incorporated at each step, but you don't want the dough to become too dry or heavy. Stop the mixer intermittently and touch the dough; it should still be tacky, but not too sticky. The dough will take anywhere from 1 to 1½ cup (5 to 7½ ounces) of additional all-purpose flour. The dough should become elastic but may not be entirely smooth because of the raisins. This kneading process will take 6 to 10 minutes.

Empty the dough out onto a well-floured surface, scrape the bowl with a pastry scraper, adding any bits of dough from the bowl to the mound, and gently knead it into a ball. Put it back into the bowl, and place a piece of plastic wrap on the surface of the dough.

Place it in a warm spot, and let it rise 1 to 1½ hours, or until doubled in bulk.

Pull back the plastic wrap, and empty the dough onto a well-floured surface. Fold the dough over, once in each direction, to release the gases. Divide the dough in 3 equal pieces; each piece will weigh roughly 1 pound, 2 ounces. Sprinkle a large baking sheet with the cornmeal. Form dough into a round (page 21), and place on the prepared baking pan. Repeat the process with the additional portions of dough.

Cover the pan gently with a tea towel or light kitchen cloth, and let the rounds rise for 45 minutes to 1 hour, or until doubled in bulk.

Arrange the oven rack in the middle of the oven, and fifteen minutes prior to baking, preheat to 375°F. Before baking, remove the tea towel and slash the loaves (page 23).

Place the pan in the center of the oven and bake for approximately 35 to 40 minutes, rotating it once at the halfway point.

Remove the rounds from the oven, and set them on a cooling rack for approximately 5 minutes. Take the loaves off the pan, return them to the rack, and allow them to cool to room temperature before enjoying.

Oatmeal Bread

OATMEAL IS NOT JUST FOR BREAKFAST CEREAL! IT CAN BE USED AS A GRAIN WHEN MAKING THIS subtly flavored wheat bread. This recipe begins by making a bowl of oatmeal. By reconstituting the oatmeal, a softer, more tender consistency is obtained while still maintaining the nutty flavor of the oats. Sweetened with honey, this wholesome bread is as good toasted in the morning (*instead* of the typical cereal) as it is sliced for sandwiches at noon.

Makes 2 loaves

1 cup (3¼ ounces) standard rolled oats,
not quick cook

¼ cup honey

2 tablespoons (1 ounce) unsalted butter,
at room temperature

2 teaspoons kosher salt

2 cups boiling water

¼ cup warm water (100° to 115°F)

2¼ teaspoons (1 package) dry yeast

Pinch of sugar

1 cup (5 ounces) whole wheat flour

2½ to 3 cups (12½ to 15 ounces) all-purpose flour

Put the oatmeal, honey, butter, and salt in a mixing bowl, and pour the boiling water over them. Stir to combine, and then set aside to cool to room temperature, about 30 minutes. The oatmeal mixture will have softened and absorbed the water.

In the bowl of a stand mixer, stir the water, yeast, and sugar together. Allow the mixture to bloom. It should become bubbly and smell yeasty, about 10 minutes.

Add the whole wheat flour, 1 cup (5 ounces) of all-purpose flour, and the oatmeal mixture to the yeast. With the paddle attachment, turn the mixer to low speed, and mix. Add 1 additional cup (5 ounces) of all-purpose flour, and continue to mix at low speed until the mixture becomes web-like and is more difficult to mix with the paddle attachment.

Understanding Gluten

Gluten has become such a hot topic these days, it would be hard to ignore it—especially when compiling a book about bread! Gluten is found in flours of all kinds (it is also *not* found in certain flours). It's most prevalent, however, in wheat flours; this is the protein that makes bread chewy and gives it its "structure." Nowadays, it seems like many people are allergic or sensitive to this protein. To those people, I have only one recommendation—just step away from this book—nothing to see here!

This protein plays an important part in making bread, maybe even *the* most important part in bread-making. Gluten lays dormant in flour. It needs the addition of liquid to activate it, and even then, it requires some work. It is a complex network of tiny fibers. When handled correctly, this network becomes smooth and stretchy. It traps air that is generated by leavening and helps to make the dough rise. For example, immediately after liquid is added to the dough, think of what it looks like and how it behaves: The dough is lumpy, and even when brought together, it may tear easily. This is because the gluten structure is low. When we mix ingredients to form and eventually knead dough, we are increasing gluten. With time and a bit of labor the dough relaxes. A dough with good gluten structure will be free of lumps. It should be elastic and smooth and respond well to touch. This shows that the ingredients have been adequately mixed and kneaded, and they have softened the tangle of proteins.

While the gluten protein is microscopic, it is reflected in the dough-making process quite simply. Through sight, touch, and a bit of practice, you will learn to work with it to make chewy and tender loaves of bread.

Remove the paddle and attach the dough hook. With the mixer on low speed, begin kneading with the dough hook, adding additional flour in ¼-cup increments. The dough will become a more cohesive mass, more elastic, and start to pull away from the sides of the bowl. It is important to watch the dough during this process. All of the flour should be incorporated at each step, but you don't want the dough to become too dry or heavy. Stop the mixer intermittently and touch the dough; it should still be tacky, but not too sticky. Dough will take anywhere from ½ to 1 cup (2½ to 5 ounces) of additional flour. While the dough will still be lumpy due to the oatmeal, it should become more elastic. This kneading process will take 6 to 10 minutes.

Empty the dough out onto a well-floured surface, scrape the bowl with a pastry scraper, adding any bits of dough from the bowl to the mound, and gently knead it into a ball. Put it into the bowl, and place a piece of plastic wrap on the surface of the dough.

Place it in a warm spot, and let it rise 1 to 1½ hours, or until doubled in bulk.

Pull back the plastic wrap, and empty the dough out onto a well-floured surface. Fold the dough over, once in each direction, to release the gases. Divide the dough in half; each half will be a little over 1 pound. Then form it into a loaf either by rolling or folding (pages 20–21). Tuck the ends under, press the seams of dough together, and place in a loaf pan. Repeat the process with the second portion of dough.

Cover the pans with plastic wrap, and let the loaves rise for an additional hour, or until doubled in bulk. The loaves should be just cresting the lip of the pan. The bread will continue to rise when baked.

Arrange the oven rack in the middle of the oven, and fifteen minutes prior to baking, preheat to 375°F.

Immediately before baking, remove the plastic wrap and slash the loaves (pages 23–24). Place the pans in the center of the oven, and bake for approximately 35 to 40 minutes, rotating the pans once at the halfway point.

Remove the loaves from the oven, and set them on a cooling rack for approximately 5 minutes. Release the loaves from the pans, and allow them to cool to room temperature before enjoying.

Hippie Bread

WHOLE WHEAT, NATURAL MEALS, AND ANCIENT GRAINS HAVE BECOME A BIT OF OBSESSION LATELY— and I can see why. These sorts of flours offer an interesting chew, a unique taste, and a hearty texture to satisfy even the hungriest of appetites. But everything old *is* new again. During the 1960s and 1970s—the *hippie* era—American diners were fixated on baking and eating whole grain breads as well. Chock full of seeds, grains, nuts, and sometimes dried fruit, these were the kind of breads that you would eat for breakfast and not have to think about food again until lunchtime.

I baked a lot of these breads hoping to come up with a recipe for this book. Many of the breads were dense—too dense; they could be dry—and rather flavorless. But they were *good* for you! Finally I have come up with just the sort of whole grain bread that I was looking for. Baked with oatmeal, pearls of crunchy millet, and sunflower seeds, with a mixture of whole wheat and all-purpose flour, this bread is soft and chewy. Sweetened with molasses and honey, the bread is both nourishing and enticing.

Makes 2 loaves

½ cup (1¾ ounces) plus I tablespoon standard rolled oats, not quick cook

½ cup (2½ ounces) plus I tablespoon unsalted sunflower seeds

¼ cup (1¾ ounces) millet

½ cup (2 ounces) wheat germ

2½ teaspoons kosher salt

2 cups hot water, from the tap is fine

2 tablespoons vegetable oil

3 tablespoons molasses

¼ cup honey

¼ cup warm water (100° to 115°F)

2¼ teaspoons (I package) dry yeast

Pinch of sugar

2½ cups (12½ ounces) whole wheat flour

2 to 2½ cups (10 to 12½ ounces) all-purpose flour

Put $\frac{1}{2}$ cup oatmeal, $\frac{1}{2}$ cup sunflower seeds, the millet, wheat germ, and salt in a mixing bowl, and pour the hot water over them. Stir in the oil, molasses, and honey to combine, and set aside to cool until warm.

In a small bowl or glass, mix the warm water, yeast, and sugar together. Allow the mixture to bloom. It should become bubbly and smell yeasty, about 10 minutes.

In the bowl of a stand mixer fitted with the paddle attachment, add the cooled grain mixture and the whole wheat flour. At low speed, mix until just combined. Add the yeast mixture, and mix briefly. Add $1\frac{1}{2}$ cups ($7\frac{1}{2}$ ounces) of all-purpose flour, and continue to mix at low speed, until the mixture is well-combined.

Remove the paddle and attach the dough hook. With the mixer on low speed, begin kneading with the dough hook, adding additional flour in $\frac{1}{4}$-cup increments. The dough will become a more cohesive mass, more elastic, and start to pull away from the sides of the bowl. It is important to watch the dough during this process. All of the flour should be incorporated at each step, but you don't want the dough to become too dry or heavy. Stop the mixer intermittently and touch the dough; it should still be tacky, but not too sticky. Dough will take anywhere from $\frac{1}{2}$ to 1 cup ($2\frac{1}{2}$ to 5 ounces) of additional all-purpose flour. It should be smooth and free of lumps of flour. This kneading process will take 6 to 10 minutes.

Empty the dough out onto a well-floured surface, scrape the bowl with a pastry scraper, adding any bits of dough from the bowl to the mound, and gently knead it into a ball. Put it back into the bowl, and place a piece of plastic wrap on the surface of the dough.

Place it in a warm spot, and let it rise 1 to $1\frac{1}{2}$ hours, or until doubled in bulk.

Pull back the plastic wrap, and empty the dough out onto a well-floured surface. Fold the dough over, once in each direction, to release the gases. Divide the dough in half; each half will be approximately 1 pound, 10 ounces. Then form into a loaf either by rolling or folding (pages 20–21). Tuck the ends under, press the seams together, and place in a loaf pan. Repeat the process with the second portion of dough.

Cover the pans with plastic wrap, and let the loaves rise for approximately 1 hour, or until doubled in bulk. The loaves should be just cresting the lip of the pan. The bread will continue to rise when baked.

Arrange the oven rack in the middle of the oven, and fifteen minutes prior to baking, preheat to 375°F.

Immediately before baking, remove the plastic wrap, and slash the loaves (pages 23–24). Brush the loaves with water, and then sprinkle the remaining tablespoons of oatmeal and sunflower seeds on top. Place the pans in the center of the oven and bake for approximately 40 to 45 minutes, rotating the pans once at the halfway point.

Remove the loaves from the oven, and set on a cooling rack for approximately 5 minutes. Release the loaves from the pans, and allow them to cool to room temperature before enjoying.

HOW DO I KNOW WHEN MY BREAD HAS PROOFED?

Sometimes when dough is placed in that warm, draft-free location to do its rising, one can forget its original size. Mixing bowls can be deceiving, and memories fleeting. How are you supposed to know if your dough has risen substantially? It is times like these that you should remember that a yeast dough is not delicate. Feel free to nudge it, or give it a poke. The dough should feel warm to the touch, and when pressed, your finger should make an indentation in the dough. If this indentation remains even after you have released your finger from the dough, you know that it has risen enough, and you can proceed with the next steps in making bread.

Jewish-Style Rye Bread or Corn Rye Bread

THIS IS THE BREAD OF JEWISH DELICATESSENS THAT DOT URBAN LANDSCAPES ACROSS AMERICA. Toasted as the accompaniment to a lox scramble, the sturdy foundation to a corned beef sandwich, or slathered with cream cheese and jam, it is delicious and ubiquitous. Growing up, when the server at the deli we frequented asked my dad what type of toast he'd like, he always would answer quickly—"Rye."

Rye was the most commonly used grain in Eastern Europe. Breads were dark, hardy, sustaining, and often seeded. When Jewish immigrants began to flood American shores during the early twentieth century they were surprised to see that rye, a grain they knew so well, had already taken root in their new home. They began to bake with this grain again in America, coating the bread with cornmeal, and often studding the dough with caraway seeds. Jewish rye bread came to be known for the licorice flavor of the seeds, but in fact, rye refers to the flour, not the caraway taste.

Often made with a sponge or a sourdough starter, this bread can also be baked as a straight dough. Made more simply with dried yeast, the straight dough method is the route I take when I want to bake Jewish Rye Bread. Using half rye flour and half all-purpose flour, this bread still maintains that nutty, whole-grain goodness, and you can make it in a matter of hours, not a matter of days, as you would have with a sourdough starter. Softened with a bit of vegetable oil, this dough bakes up moist and chewy. Toasted, it's sublime.

If you decide that you don't appreciate the caraway flavor, omit the seeds, and bake the Corn Rye Bread instead.

Makes 1 round

1 cup warm water (100° to 115°F)

2¼ teaspoons (1 package) dry yeast

1 tablespoon sugar

1 cup (5 ounces) dark rye flour

3 tablespoons vegetable oil

2 teaspoons kosher salt

{Ingredients continue on next page}

1¼ to 1¾ cups (6¼ to 8¾ ounces) all-purpose flour

1 tablespoon caraway seed (optional)

1½ teaspoons cornmeal

In the bowl of a stand mixer, mix the water, yeast, and sugar together. Allow the mixture to bloom. It should become bubbly and smell yeasty, about 10 minutes. Mix in the rye flour, and allow the mixture to stand for 20 minutes. This step allows the rye flour to fully hydrate.

Add the oil, salt, and 1 cup (5 ounces) of all-purpose flour, and using the paddle attachment on low speed, mix briefly until combined.

Remove the paddle and attach the dough hook. With the mixer on low speed, begin kneading with the dough hook and adding the additional flour a few tablespoons at a time. The dough will become a more cohesive mass, more elastic, and start to pull away from the sides of the bowl. It is important to watch the dough during this process. All of the flour should be incorporated at each step, but you don't want the dough to become too dry or heavy. Rye flour is a sticky flour to work with. The dough will still remain quite sticky, but the kneading process will become easier and the dough, smoother. This kneading process will take 5 to 8 minutes.

Empty the dough out onto a well-floured surface, scrape the bowl with a pastry scraper, adding any bits of dough from the bowl to the mound, and gently knead it into a ball. Put it back into the bowl, and place a piece of plastic wrap on the surface of the dough.

Place it in a warm spot, and let it rise 1 to 1½ hours, or until doubled in bulk.

Pull back the plastic wrap, and empty the dough out onto a well-floured surface. Fold the dough over, once in each direction, to release the gases. Form the dough into a round (pages 22–23), and place it on a baking pan. Cover the pan gently with a tea towel or light kitchen cloth, and let the round rise for 45 minutes to 1 hour, or until doubled in bulk.

Arrange the oven rack in the middle of the oven, and fifteen minutes prior to baking, preheat to 350°F. Before baking, remove the tea towel, mist with water, sprinkle with cornmeal, and slash the loaves (pages 23–24).

Place the pan in the center of the oven and bake for approximately 40 to 45 minutes, rotating the pan once at the halfway point.

Remove the bread from the oven, and set it on a cooling rack for approximately 5 minutes. Take the loaf off the pan, return it to the rack, and allow it to cool to room temperature before enjoying.

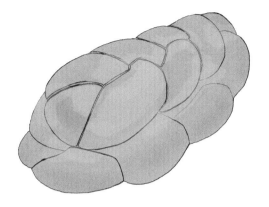

Challah

CHALLAH IS A BRAIDED, CELEBRATORY, JEWISH BREAD. THE BREAD IS SLIGHTLY SWEET, SYMBOLIZING the sweetness of life; at times it is studded with raisins or sprinkled with seeds. You'll see most challahs braided, either intricately or with a simple three-strand braid. It all varies—but this rich bread is always made supple with oil and never butter, to maintain the Kosher laws of not mixing meat with milk. By using oil, Kosher Jews can enjoy a slice of bread while still having meat in their meals.

Tinged a golden yellow and rich with eggs, this bread makes wonderful French toast and bread pudding. Used in diners and delis alike, this bread has now become almost as ubiquitous as a standard white bread in America's dining tradition. This recipe uses a sponge—a yeast and flour mixture that is left to bloom and ferment slightly—before making the final dough. Using a sponge will give the bread a rounder, more full-bodied flavor. When kneading the dough, you will notice that it is tighter and stiffer. The end result will be a finer crumb and a softer bread.

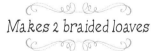

Makes 2 braided loaves

SPONGE:

⅓ cup warm water (100° to 115°F)

2¼ teaspoons (1 package) dry yeast

½ cup (2½ ounces) all-purpose flour

{Ingredients continue on next page}

DOUGH:

All of the sponge

2 eggs

1 egg yolk

1 cup warm water (100° to 115°F)

½ cup vegetable oil

⅓ cup sugar

2 teaspoons salt

4½ to 5 cups (1 pound, 6½ ounces to
1 pound, 9 ounces) all-purpose flour

1 egg

To make the sponge: In the bowl of a stand mixer, stir the water, yeast, and flour together until combined. Cover with plastic wrap, and let it rest at room temperature for 15 minutes. The mixture should become bubbly and smell yeasty.

To make the dough: In the same bowl of the stand mixer fitted with a paddle attachment, add the eggs, egg yolk, water, oil, sugar, salt, and 3 cups (15 ounces) of flour to the sponge. At low speed, mix until combined. The mixture will be become web-like and be more difficult to mix with the paddle attachment. This may require an additional ½ cup of flour.

Remove the paddle and attach the dough hook. With the mixer on low speed, begin kneading with the dough hook and adding additional flour in ¼- to ½-cup increments. The dough will become a more cohesive mass, more elastic, and start to pull away from the sides of the bowl. It is important to watch the dough during this process. All of the flour should be incorporated at each step, but you don't want the dough to become too dry or heavy. The dough will take anywhere from 1½ to 2 cups (7½ to 10 ounces) of additional flour. It should be smooth and free of lumps. This kneading process will take 6 to 10 minutes.

Empty the dough out onto a well-floured surface, scrape the bowl with a pastry scraper, adding any bits of dough from the bowl to the mound, and gently knead it into a ball. Put it back into the bowl, and place a piece of plastic wrap on the surface of the dough.

Place it in a warm spot, and let the dough rise 1 to 1½ hours, or until doubled in bulk.

Pull back the plastic wrap, and empty the dough out onto a well-floured surface. Fold the dough over, once in each direction, to release the gases. Divide the dough in half, and let the dough rest for 5 minutes, to relax the glutens. Separate the dough into 6 pieces, roughly the same size.

Work on forming one challah at a time. Roll 3 strands into cylinders, approximately 12 to 15 inches long. If you are having trouble forming a strand, leave the dough for a moment to relax the glutens, and return to it later. This process may need to be repeated several times when forming the strands for the braid. When strands are created, lay them parallel to each other, on a parchment-lined baking sheet. Begin braiding from the center of the strands and work your way to the ends; this will help maintain a consistent width. Press the ends of the braid together, and tuck them under. Repeat with other strands to form another braid. You will be able to fit both braids on one large baking sheet.

Grease a piece of plastic wrap with oil, cover the braids with the wrap, and let them rise for about 1 hour, or until doubled in bulk.

Arrange the oven rack in the middle of the oven, and fifteen minutes prior to baking, preheat to 375°F.

In a small bowl, prepare the egg wash by beating the egg and 1 tablespoon water together. Remove the plastic wrap, and brush the challahs with egg wash.

Place the pan in the center of the oven and bake for approximately 40 minutes.

Remove the pan from the oven, and set it on a cooling rack for approximately 5 minutes. Take the loaves off the pan, return them to the rack, and allow them to cool to room temperature before enjoying.

Potato Bread

IN AMERICA, WOMEN HAVE BEEN MAKING POTATO BREADS FOR AS LONG AS THERE HAVE BEEN POTA-toes to cook. By mashing or ricing a boiled, starchy potato, adding it to the flour mixture, and then using the potato-cooking water in the dough, a supremely moist, chewy bread is made. Tastiness aside, I think this type of bread has been so popular for another reason—it's relatively quick. The potato and its cooking water contain starches and sugars that the yeast loves. It will proof in no time, and the yeast will keep feeding and working throughout the rising process. Depending on the weather conditions, you will find that the preparation time can be reduced by as much as one hour. The dough will be buoyant, if a little unruly, but the airiness translates into one light and delicious loaf of bread.

This bread is a wonderful substitute for the Basic White Loaf (page 26) or the Buttermilk Bread (page 30). If you're in the mood for a more savory loaf, you'll find it in the Potato-Onion Rounds (page 52).

Makes 2 loaves

1 medium Russet potato (8 to 10 ounces),
peeled, cut into 1-inch chunks

1½ cups potato cooking water

2¼ teaspoons (1 package) dry yeast

3 tablespoons (1½ ounces) unsalted butter,
at room temperature

1 tablespoon sugar

1 tablespoon kosher salt

4 to 4½ cups (1 pound, 4 ounces to 1 pound,
6½ ounces) all-purpose flour

In a medium-sized saucepan, boil the potato in 3 cups of water for about 15 minutes, or until very soft. Drain the potato, reserving the cooking water. With a potato masher or a ricer, mash the potato until it's smooth and no lumps remain. Set the mashed potato and the cooking water aside to cool to 110° to 120°F.

In the bowl of a stand mixer fitted with the paddle attachment, add 1½ cups of cooled potato-cooking water and the yeast. Stir to combine, and allow the mixture to bloom. It should become bubbly and smell yeasty, about 5 minutes. Add the mashed potato, butter, sugar, salt, and 3 cups (15 ounces) of flour to the yeast mixture. Mix at low speed until the mixture becomes web-like and more difficult to mix with the paddle attachment.

Remove the paddle and attach the dough hook. With the mixer on low speed, begin kneading with the dough hook, adding additional flour in $\frac{1}{4}$- to $\frac{1}{2}$-cup increments. The dough will become a more cohesive mass, more elastic, and start to pull away from the sides of the bowl. It is important to watch the dough during this process. All of the flour should be incorporated at each step, but you don't want the dough to become too dry or heavy. Stop the mixer intermittently and touch the dough; it should still be tacky, but not too sticky. The dough will take anywhere from 1 to $1\frac{1}{2}$ cups (5 to $7\frac{1}{2}$ ounces) of additional flour. It should be smooth and free of lumps. This kneading process will take 6 to 10 minutes.

Empty the dough out onto a well-floured surface, scrape the bowl with a pastry scraper, adding any bits of dough from the bowl to the mound, and gently knead it into a ball. Put it back into the bowl, and place a piece of plastic wrap on the surface of the dough.

Place it in a warm spot, and let the dough rise 1 to $1\frac{1}{2}$ hours, or until doubled in bulk.

Pull back the plastic wrap, and empty the dough out onto a well-floured surface. Fold the dough over, once in each direction, to release the gases. Divide the dough in half; each half will be a little over 1 pound. Then form it into a loaf either by rolling or folding (page 000). Tuck the ends under, press the seams together, and place in a loaf pan. Repeat the process with the second portion of dough.

Cover the pans with plastic wrap, and let the loaves rise for 45 minutes to 1 hour, or until doubled in bulk. The loaves should be just cresting the lip of the pan. The bread will continue to rise when baked.

Arrange the oven rack in the middle of the oven, and fifteen minutes prior to baking, preheat to 400°F.

Immediately before baking, remove the plastic wrap, and slash the loaves (pages 23–24). Place the pans in the center of the oven and bake for approximately 35 to 40 minutes, rotating the pans once at the halfway point.

Remove the loaves from the oven, and set them on a cooling rack for approximately 5 minutes. Release the loaves from the pans, and allow them to cool to room temperature before enjoying.

Potato-Onion Rounds

IF YOU ARE LOOKING FOR A MORE SAVORY TAKE ON THE TRADITIONAL POTATO BREAD, THESE ROUNDS fit the bill. Adorned with poppy seeds and seasoned with sautéed onion, these shiny rounds taste like a bagel and are chewy and soft, almost like an egg bread—without the egg. The bread is a tasty accompaniment for soups and stews and makes a delicious grilled cheese sandwich the day after it's baked.

Makes 2 rounds

1 tablespoon olive oil

1 large yellow onion, diced

Salt and pepper, to taste

1 recipe Potato Bread (page 50)

1 tablespoon coarsely ground cornmeal

1 egg

¾ teaspoon poppy seeds

In a medium-sized skillet, over medium heat, heat the olive oil until shimmering. Add the onion, season with salt and pepper, and sauté until the onion becomes translucent and the volume reduces by about one-half, about 3 to 5 minutes. Scrape the onions into a bowl, and set aside to cool.

Proceed with the recipe for the Potato Bread through the kneading in the stand mixer. Empty the dough onto a well-floured surface. Add about half of the cooled onion to the dough, and begin to knead by hand. When this portion is mixed, add the rest of the onions, and continue to knead until the dough is smooth and onion is well-combined. Form the dough into a ball, put it back into the bowl, and place a piece of plastic wrap on the surface of the dough.

Place it in a warm spot, and let the dough rise 1 to 1½ hours, or until doubled in bulk.

Pull back the plastic wrap, and empty the dough out onto a well-floured surface. Fold the dough over, once in each direction, to release the gases. Divide the dough in half; each half will be approximately 1½ pounds. Sprinkle a large baking pan with the cornmeal. Form the dough into a round (page 21), and place it on the prepared baking pan. Repeat the process with the second portion of dough.

Cover the pan gently with a tea towel or light kitchen cloth, and let the rounds rise for 45 minutes to 1 hour, or until doubled in bulk.

Arrange the oven rack in the middle of the oven, and fifteen minutes prior to baking, preheat to 400°F.

In a small bowl, mix the egg and 1 tablespoon water together. Remove the tea towel, and brush the egg wash on the rounds, then sprinkle with the poppy seeds. Slash the rounds (pages 22–23).

Place the pan in the center of the oven and bake for approximately 35 to 40 minutes, rotating the pan once at the halfway point.

Remove the pan from the oven, and set it on a cooling rack for approximately 5 minutes. Take the rounds off the pan, return them to the rack, and allow them to cool to room temperature before enjoying.

Mica's Bread

KINGSTON IS A QUAINT TOWN ALONG THE HUDSON RIVER NEAR WOODSTOCK, NEW YORK. IT HAS A small-town vibe, and the downtown, lined with old storefronts and row houses, has quite a vibrant food scene for an otherwise sleepy village. In the Uptown District stands Duo Bistro, a slim restaurant with a pared down aesthetic, a sturdy front bar, and amazing food. While traveling through town, I stopped here for brunch. I ordered a stick-to-your-ribs hash of turkey confit (I would highly recommend this dish to anyone traveling through) that came with a side of toast. However, this wasn't just your average bread. It was hearty, rustic, slightly sweet—and perfectly toasted. One taste, and I knew the recipe would have to be included in this book.

I talked to the chef and co-owner of the restaurant, Juan Romero, who bakes the bread on the premises. The bread, named after his son Mica, was his creation. Mica was born while Juan was opening the restaurant. He wanted a bread that was different and nourishing, with an easy-to-follow recipe that could be produced by virtually anyone. The unique part of this recipe is that it is a straight dough—meaning that all of the ingredients are mixed at once. This bread also has only one rise, something that you would never guess upon tasting its complexity. The bread has such a well-developed structure and nutty taste; it's the type of bread that stays with you all day. And the single rise makes it quick; it can be assembled, baked, and put to use all in one morning.

The recipe and kneading times are quite specific. The dough is heavy; it will give your mixer a workout. Just when you think that this lump of flour and water won't come together, they form a beautiful, elastic dough. Mica's Bread shows that that the tradition of masterful American bread baking is alive and well in the United States.

Makes 2 rounds

2⅓ cups warm water (100° to 115°F)

½ cup molasses

1 tablespoon dry yeast

2 cups (10 ounces) all-purpose flour

2 cups (10 ounces) high-gluten bread flour

1¾ cups (8¾ ounces) whole wheat flour

1 cup (3¼ ounces) standard rolled oats, not quick cook

½ cup (2½ ounces) roasted, unsalted sunflower seeds

I tablespoon kosher salt

In a medium-size bowl, mix the water, molasses, and yeast together. Allow the mixture to bloom. It should become bubbly and smell yeasty, about 10 minutes.

In the bowl of a stand mixer, add the flours, oats, sunflower seeds, and salt. Briefly turn on the mixer just to combine the ingredients. All at once, add the yeast mixture, and mix on low speed with the dough hook attachment for 10 minutes. The dough will turn from a shaggy mass into a more cohesive product during the mixing process. Allow the dough to rest for 5 minutes, to allow for the glutens to relax. Mix again, on low speed, for 7 minutes. The dough will become smoother and more elastic.

Empty the dough onto a floured work surface. Divide it into two equal portions. The dough will be quite dry, so little-to-no flour is needed for forming. Form each portion into a round (page 21). Place them on a well-floured baking pan, and cover gently with a tea towel or light kitchen cloth. Place the rounds in a warm spot, and let them rise until doubled in bulk; this may take more than 1 hour, depending on room temperature.

Arrange the oven rack in the middle of the oven, and fifteen minutes prior to baking, preheat to 375°F.

Remove the tea towel from the pan, and slash the rounds (pages 23–24). If desired, mist or brush the surface of the dough with water, and sprinkle with more oats. Place the pan in the center of the oven and bake for approximately 45 to 50 minutes, rotating the pan once at the halfway point. The rounds will be golden brown.

Remove the pan from the oven, and set it on a cooling rack for approximately 5 minutes. Take the rounds off the pan, return them to the rack, and allow them to cool to room temperature before enjoying.

Soft Brown Bread with Grits

BREADS WERE NOT ALWAYS MADE WITH FLOUR ALONE. HISTORICALLY, WHEAT FLOUR WAS AN EXPEN-sive, prized ingredient, so women made do with other meals and flours when baking bread. They used cornmeal, cooked rice, coarse wheat or rye flours, or in the case of this moist loaf—grits.

I have adapted this recipe from the 1894 book *Maryland and Virginia Cook Book* by Mrs. Charles H. Gibson, where she instructs her readers to use a "teacupful" of boiled grits saved from the morning's breakfast. Her "making do" recipe makes one delicious homestyle bread, perfect for sandwiches of all kinds.

Makes 2 loaves

½ cup (3 ounces) old fashioned grits, not instant or quick-cooking

2 tablespoons (1 ounce) unsalted butter

3 tablespoons honey

¼ cup warm water (100° to 115°F)

3 teaspoons dry yeast

Pinch of sugar

1½ cups whole milk, at room temperature

2 teaspoons kosher salt

2 cups (10 ounces) whole wheat flour

1½ to 2 cups (7½ to 10 ounces) all-purpose flour

In a medium-sized saucepan, bring 1½ cups of water to a boil. Slowly add the grits, turn the heat to simmer, and cover. Stirring occasionally to make sure that grits are not sticking to the bottom of the pan, cook for 10 minutes. All of the liquid should be absorbed, and grits should be thickened to the consistency of oatmeal. Mix in the butter and the honey until the butter is melted. Turn off the heat, and let the grits cool to room temperature, approximately 20 minutes.

In a small bowl or glass, mix the water, yeast, and sugar together. Allow the mixture to bloom. It should become bubbly and smell yeasty, about 10 minutes.

In the bowl of a stand mixer fitted with the paddle attachment, add the grits, milk, salt, and the whole wheat flour. At low speed, mix until just combined. Add the yeast mixture, and mix briefly. Add $\frac{1}{2}$ cup ($2\frac{1}{2}$ ounces) of all-purpose flour, and continue to mix at low speed until mixture becomes web-like and becomes more difficult to mix with the paddle attachment.

Remove the paddle and attach the dough hook. With the mixer on low speed, begin kneading with the dough hook, adding additional flour in $\frac{1}{4}$- to $\frac{1}{2}$-cup increments. The dough will become a more cohesive mass, more elastic, and start to pull away from the sides of the bowl. It is important to watch the dough during this process. All of the flour should be incorporated at each step, but you don't want the dough to become too dry or heavy. Stop the mixer intermittently and touch the dough; it should still be tacky, but not too sticky. The dough will take anywhere from 1 to $1\frac{1}{2}$ cups (5 to $7\frac{1}{2}$ ounces) of additional all-purpose flour. It should be smooth and free of lumps. This kneading process will take 6 to 10 minutes.

Empty the dough out onto a well-floured surface, scrape the bowl with a pastry scraper, adding any bits of dough from the bowl to the mound, and gently knead it into a ball. Put it back into the bowl, and place a piece of plastic wrap on the surface of the dough.

Place it in a warm spot, and let it rise 1 to $1\frac{1}{2}$ hours, or until doubled in bulk.

Pull back the plastic wrap, and empty the dough out onto a well-floured surface. Fold the dough over, once in each direction, to release the gases. Divide the dough in half; each half will be approximately $1\frac{1}{2}$ pounds. Form it into a loaf either by rolling or folding (pages 20–21). Tuck the ends under, press the seams of dough together, and place in a loaf pan. Repeat the process with the second portion of dough.

Cover the pans with plastic wrap, and let the loaves rise for approximately 1 hour, or until doubled in bulk. The loaves should be just cresting the lip of the pan. The bread will continue to rise when baked.

Arrange the oven rack in the middle of the oven, and fifteen minutes prior to baking, preheat to 375°F.

Immediately before baking, remove the plastic wrap, and slash the loaves (pages 23–24). Place the pans in the center of the oven and bake for approximately 40 to 45 minutes, rotating pans once at the halfway point.

Remove the loaves from the oven, and set them on a cooling rack for approximately 5 minutes. Release the loaves from the pans, and allow them to cool to room temperature before enjoying.

Amish Dill Bread

RICH AND WHOLESOME, THIS BREAD HAS BEEN A MAINSTAY IN AMISH KITCHENS FOR YEARS. THE addition of cottage cheese is a smooth and almost luxurious balance for the unique, herbaceous taste of the dill weed.

Many of the Amish baked goods tend to be quite sweet, even those with a savory bent, so I have cut back on the sugar. This way, the true dairy richness of the cottage cheese is able to come through. When you are kneading the dough, you will notice it is not completely smooth. Small pockets of cottage cheese curds remain intact, and upon baking, lend a richness to the bread that can't be beat.

I favor using fresh dill in this recipe, but in a pinch, you can use the dried variety. Simply cut back the amount to one teaspoon.

Makes 1 loaf

¼ cup lukewarm water (105° to 115°F)

2¼ teaspoons (1 package) dry yeast

Pinch of sugar

1 cup cottage cheese, heated to lukewarm

1 egg

2 tablespoons fresh dill, minced

2 tablespoons finely minced onion (see note)

1 tablespoon (½ ounce) unsalted butter,
at room temperature

1 tablespoon sugar

1 teaspoon kosher salt

2 to 2½ cups (10 to 12½ ounces) all-purpose flour

In a small bowl or glass, mix the water, yeast, and sugar together. Allow the mixture to bloom. It should become bubbly and smell yeasty, about 10 minutes.

In the bowl of a stand mixer fitted with the paddle attachment, add the cottage cheese, egg, dill, onion, butter, sugar, salt, and 1 cup (5 ounces) of the flour. At low speed, mix until just combined. Add the yeast mixture, and mix briefly. Add another ½ cup (2½ ounces) of flour, and continue to mix at low speed until mixture becomes web-like and more difficult to mix with the paddle attachment.

Remove the paddle and attach the dough hook. With the mixer on low speed, begin kneading with the dough hook, adding additional flour in $\frac{1}{4}$-cup increments. The dough will become a more cohesive mass, more elastic, and start to pull away from the sides of the bowl. It is important to watch the dough during this process. All of the flour should be incorporated at each step, but you don't want the dough to become too dry or heavy. Stop the mixer intermittently and touch the dough; it should still be tacky, but not too sticky. The dough will take anywhere from $\frac{1}{2}$ to 1 cup ($2\frac{1}{2}$ to 5 ounces) of additional flour. It should be smooth, but some lumps will remain due to the cottage cheese. This kneading process will take 6 to 10 minutes.

Empty the dough out onto a well-floured surface, scrape the bowl with a pastry scraper, adding any bits of dough from the bowl to the mound, and gently knead it into a ball. Put it back into the bowl, and place a piece of plastic wrap on the surface of the dough.

Place it in a warm spot, and let it rise for approximately 1 hour, or until doubled in bulk.

Pull back the plastic wrap, and empty the dough out onto a well-floured surface. Fold the dough over, once in each direction, to release the gases. Then form it into a loaf either by rolling or folding (pages 20–21). Tuck the ends under, press the seams of dough together, and place in a loaf pan.

Cover the pan with plastic wrap, and let the loaf rise for 1 hour, or until doubled in bulk. The loaf should be just cresting the lip of the pan. The bread will continue to rise when baked.

Arrange the oven rack in the middle of the oven, and 15 minutes prior to baking, preheat to 350°F.

Immediately before baking, remove the plastic wrap, and slash the loaf (pages 23–24). Place the pan in the center of the oven and bake for approximately 40 to 45 minutes, rotating the pan once at the halfway point.

Remove the loaf from the oven, and set on a cooling rack for approximately 5 minutes. Release the loaf from the pan, and allow it to cool to room temperature before enjoying.

NOTE: Rather than finely mincing the onion, you may choose to grate it. Running a peeled onion along the side of a box grater will both process the onion and emit the juice.

Pullman Loaf

I AM NOT THE SORT OF COOK WHO HAS A LOT OF KITCHEN GADGETS OR SPECIALTY PANS. THEY JUST take up precious counter space, and I make do with the basics. But the one "gadget" I make an exception for is my Pullman Loaf bread pan. Maybe you have seen this long bread pan with its sharply angled corners, its squared off sides, and sliding metal lid. The pan looks a bit like a casket—for bread, of course! It makes the most perfect loaf of bread, with a tight crumb and a well-trained crust. The name is said to derive from the days when railroad travel was king, and George Pullman, who developed the Pullman railway cars, needed a sandwich loaf that economized space in his petite dining cars. By baking a long loaf of bread without the typical bulbous top, he was able to almost double the amount of bread slices in a single loaf. His Pullman Company is credited with inventing this ingenious pan. Because of the lid, the dough is contained during the baking process, and a perfect rectangle of bread is produced. These could be stacked like bricks in the dining car. A slice of Pullman Bread is ideal for dainty sandwiches, but makes wonderful French toast, and the neutral, dairy-rich flavor makes a delicious bread pudding, too. And the bread is so long, you will surely have enough for all three options!

Makes 1 13 x 4-inch Pullman loaf

¼ cup warm water (100° to 115°F)

2¼ teaspoons (1 package) dry yeast

Pinch of sugar

1⅔ cups whole milk, at room temperature

6 tablespoons (3 ounces) unsalted butter, at room temperature,
plus 1 tablespoon (½ ounce) unsalted butter,
melted, for greasing the pan

2 tablespoons honey

2 teaspoons kosher salt

4½ to 5 cups (1 pound, 6½ ounces to 1 pound, 9 ounces)
all-purpose flour

In a small bowl or glass, mix the water, yeast, and sugar together. Allow the mixture to bloom. It should become bubbly and smell yeasty, about 10 minutes.

In the bowl of a stand mixer fitted with the paddle attachment, add the milk, butter, honey, salt, and 4 cups (1 pound 4 ounces) of flour. At low speed, mix until just combined. Add the yeast mixture, and mix briefly.

Remove the paddle and attach the dough hook. With the mixer on low speed, begin kneading with the dough hook, adding additional flour in $1/4$-cup increments. The dough will become a more cohesive mass, more elastic, and start to pull away from the sides of the bowl. It is important to watch the dough during this process. All of the flour should be incorporated at each step, but you don't want the dough to become too dry or heavy. Stop the mixer intermittently and touch the dough; it should still be tacky, but not too sticky. The dough will take anywhere from $1/2$ cup to 1 cup ($2\,1/2$ to 5 ounces) of additional flour. It should be smooth and free of lumps. This kneading process will take 6 to 10 minutes.

Empty the dough out onto a well-floured surface, scrape the bowl with a pastry scraper, adding any bits of dough from the bowl to the mound, and gently knead it into a ball. Put it back into the bowl, and place a piece of plastic wrap on the surface of the dough.

Place it in a warm spot, and let the dough rise $1\,1/2$ to 2 hours, or until doubled in bulk. Brush the additional tablespoon of butter ($1/2$ ounce) onto the interior of the bread pan and the lid. Set aside.

Pull back the plastic wrap, and empty the dough out onto a lightly floured surface. Because of the large amount of butter, the dough should not be too sticky. Fold the dough over, once in each direction, to release the gases. With the heel of your hand, flatten the dough out to approximately 14 x 8 inches. Roll the dough tightly to create a cylinder, and pinch the seams closed. Tuck in the ends, and place it into the loaf pan.

Cover the pan with plastic wrap, and let the loaf rise for about 1 hour, or until the dough has risen to 1 inch under the lip of the pan.

Arrange the oven rack in the middle of the oven, and fifteen minutes prior to baking, preheat to 375°F.

Remove the plastic wrap, and slide on the cover. Place the pan in the center of the oven and bake for approximately 40 minutes, rotating once at the halfway point.

Remove the loaf from the oven, slide off the cover, and set on a cooling rack for approximately 5 minutes. Release the loaf from the pan, and allow it to cool to room temperature before enjoying.

SOURDOUGH BREAD

I GREW UP WITH SOURDOUGH. BEING FROM THE SAN FRANCISCO BAY AREA meant that sourdough bread was as common as Wonder Bread in the grocery store. Of course, this was often the mediocre grocery store bread, sealed in a plastic bag, complete with spongy crust, and pre-sliced into equal portions—but it was still sour. In addition, bakeries would offer sourdough baguettes, dinner rolls, rounds, even English muffins. There were sourdough loaves sprinkled with cheese, whole wheat loaves, rounds studded with cranberries, or speckled with herbs. What was available using straight doughs was almost always equaled in sourdough as well.

It wasn't until I moved to Manhattan that I realized that this particular sourdough childhood was not so common. I was a product of my culinary surroundings—and I longed for the type of sourdough bread that I grew up with. When I purchased my first sourdough bread in Morningside Heights and walked the few blocks home to my miniscule apartment, I sliced into the loaf and got ready to take my first bite, unmarred by even a slathering of butter. The most that I can say about that premier slice is, "Meh." It was dark, more like whole wheat than straight sourdough, and the tang was so subtle, it was almost imperceptible. But that was many years ago. I've since eaten a lot more bread on the East Coast, and some has been great. But I still longed for that true sourdough.

Having grown up with superb bakery sourdough bread, I never had a need to learn how to produce it at home. But when I decided to write this book, I knew that it would never be complete without a chapter on sourdough.

True sourdough comes from fermentation of natural yeast—not commercial (i.e., the dry yeast used in most home yeast bread recipes). This dough is what is called a perpetuating dough—meaning a small portion of the dough, which contains the yeast, must always be held aside when baking a loaf of bread. It is a living, breathing thing, needing to be fed and put to use in order to survive. If you have ever talked sourdough with people—and believe me, I have spoken to more than a few—you'll meet people whose sourdough starter is years, even decades, old. Maybe it was gifted to them by a grandparent or a friend; maybe a baker gave it to them with instructions for care and how to make a stunning loaf of bread. In essence, some people can make sourdough bread, but they can't make the starter.

What I needed was a trustworthy, reliable starter recipe in order to make a coveted loaf of bread. And so it began . . .

As I read more about sourdough starters—and due to my obsessive nature, I read *a lot*—I became slightly terrified. You know that saying, knowledge is power? Well in this case, knowledge was just dizzying. Every book had something different to say. There were starters made with organic grapes, some with pineapple juice, some with rye flour, some with all-purpose. Some made their starters in a crock, others in a stainless steel bowl, while others warned that stainless steel would kill the yeast. Some recipes claimed the yeasts were airborne and recommended beginning the starter, lid off, in one room. If no yeast seemed to be forming, you were out of luck and needed to change locales. My head became overloaded with information. What started as a simple endeavor had grown to terrifying proportions.

Sourdough seems to be mythologized. This elusive wild yeast, while intriguing, seemed impossible to capture. At one point in my trials, I had four different vats of starter slowly growing in the second bedroom of my house. It smelled like a sweat sock, and not a single starter was producing a loaf of bread that I would feed to a dinner guest, let alone include in this book. I was getting discouraged.

So I did some more reading about wild yeast and sourdough cultures. Wild yeasts exist in many places: in the air, on grains, and on fruits and vegetables, to name a few. However, this does not mean that we can produce a sourdough loaf out of thin air. The most reliable method, I discovered, is to rely on the flour to produce yeast. Every ounce of flour contains tens of thousands of cells of natural yeast; therefore it's necessary to harvest this yeast. Because this is naturally occurring yeast, sourdough does have regional differences. We all know that it is tangy in San Francisco. It may be more mild in Wisconsin, more wheaty in Vermont. This is because the *lactobacillus*, the bacteria that gives sourdough bread its characteristic sour taste, comes in various strains. But it will always be *sourdough*.

Sourdough starters can be intimidating. They can be daunting. Finicky even. But they don't have to be, and they shouldn't be. In its simplest form, a sourdough starter is simply flour and water. That's it. No yeast, no added flavoring, no added fat— just a mixture of these two basic ingredients. These doughs are what you would call "lean doughs."

After many trials, many false starts, and many vats of sour-smelling combinations of yeast and flour, I came up with a *simple* starter recipe. It is stress-free, easy to make and to maintain, and produces a delicious loaf of bread. To some, it may seem an oversimplification, but sometimes it is the most simple of things that create the most sublime results.

I like to think of my sourdough starter as a very low-maintenance pet—like a sea monkey. You have to be mindful of it and check in on it from time to time. You have to feed it. But that's about it!

Here are just a few more pieces of information to get you started on the road to sourdough: First, since the starter has just two ingredients, flour and water, make sure that your flour is high-quality. I use King Arthur Unbleached All-Purpose. Don't use bleached flour. Bleached flour strips nutrients (re: yeast) from the wheat.

Second, high-gluten flour, or bread flour, also shouldn't be used. Because it is higher in gluten protein, it is lower in starch, which is the vital nutrient provided to your starter.

Finally, some city municipalities chlorinate their drinking water. Depending on the level of chlorine, this can also hinder sourdough production. To be safe, use non-chlorinated water. Water from a Brita or other home filtration system works well, or you can use bottled water. If you choose bottled water, do not use *distilled water*; the complete lack of minerals found in this water will eventually starve your starter.

SOURDOUGH STARTER

Congratulations! You've decided to take on sourdough bread! You won't be sorry. The process of creating a viable sourdough starter will take about one week. To make a loaf of bread—three days.

Before you slam this book closed, muttering to yourself that you have a life, let me tell you, I created this three-day process with just that in mind. The time spent is largely inactive. The three days is spent waiting for fermentation and an adequate rise. The bread will have the perfect balance of sour and tang, the crust will be crunchy, the interior cool and chewy, and remember, you will not have to use *any* commercial yeasts to get these qualities. You also will waste very little flour.

Most recipes for sourdough have you discard quite a bit of flour in the building and maintenance of a starter. Each day you discard half of the starter and add a mixture of fresh flour and water. This process is to ensure a productive yeast is being made. By discarding half of the starter and adding fresh ingredients, you are essentially making the mature starter work harder to ferment the new starter. Back in the day, this old starter wasn't discarded—it was used to make a new loaf of bread. There were more mouths to feed, more bread needed to be baked, and fresh loaves were produced *daily*. Now, not so much. Most people are weekend bakers, and most families don't go through a loaf of bread a day. So, many modern-day recipes discard, rather than use, mature starters. As much as I love sourdough bread and wanted my very own starter, this always seemed so wasteful to me. When I came upon this recipe for sourdough starter on YouTube, from the husband-and-wife team of Erik Knutzen and Kelly Coyne, authors and urban homesteaders, it solved the problem of excessive discarding.

This recipe makes a small amount of starter that you feed and keep alive. The work is very minimal. With such a wee amount of starter, it is necessary to spend an additional day growing the starter into a larger portion of sponge—the dough that will eventually make a loaf of bread. Again, there is almost no work in doing this; it just requires a day of waiting. The rest of the ingredients are then added to the sponge to make a loaf of bread.

The recipes that follow the starter recipe are for a variety of breads, all which will require the same, larger portion of sourdough sponge.

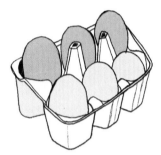

Sourdough Starter

TOOLS:

1 pint-size jar

INGREDIENTS:

7 tablespoons all-purpose flour, separated

7 tablespoons non-chlorinated water, separated

On day one, in the jar, mix one tablespoon flour, and one tablespoon water. Stir until combined, cover the jar, and place on the kitchen counter or someplace with a fairly warm and even temperature. Leave it for approximately 24 hours. I do my feedings in the morning. This seems to work best, and then you can get on with your day, go to work, etc.

AUTOLYSE

Autolyse is the technical, bread bakers' term of letting the ingredients rest without the addition of salt. When making sourdough bread, autolyse occurs when the sponge, additional flours, and water are mixed together. It is not important that these ingredients be thoroughly combined. Then leave these ingredients to rest for a minimum of 20 minutes (some bakers will leave the dough for up to one hour). This time allows for the flour to completely absorb the water and begin to develop glutens. The waiting is done prior to adding any salt, because once salt is added, the dough begins to tighten, and the glutens become stronger and more dense.

You will notice that well-rested dough is easier to work with. What once was streaky and rather dry-looking will be more fluid. The contents of the bowl will begin to look more like dough, rather than just some ingredients haphazardly thrown together. You will see that the flour has become more hydrated. The dough will require less kneading, and it will hold its shape better. Just these few moments of time will give you a loaf with a more open crumb, as well as a more delicious taste.

On day two, uncover the jar, remove approximately half of the mixture (precise measurements are not necessary), add one additional tablespoon flour and one tablespoon water. Stir until combined, cover the jar, and leave on the counter for approximately 24 hours.

You will repeat this process, of discarding and adding additional flour and water, for one week total. The mixture will become looser in the successive days. It should also begin to bubble and smell sour, or faintly of alcohol. These are the desired effects, and they mean that the process is working.

After seven days, you should have a viable starter. You maintain your starter by continuing with the discarding process. This can go on interminably. If you know someone with a starter, they may tell you that it is generations old. Yours could get to be, too!

If keeping your starter alive on the counter gets to be more than you can handle, or if you go away for a while, the jar can easily be stored in the refrigerator. Simply feed the starter, wait a few hours until it begins to work and becomes bubbly, and then put it in the refrigerator. When you are ready to revive this dormant starter, remove it from the refrigerator, leave it out overnight, and then begin the discarding and feeding ritual the next day. A dormant starter will need at least two days of feeding to make sure that the yeast is strong enough before making the sourdough sponge.

There are times when your starter may smell overwhelmingly of alcohol, and the paste may appear too thin and watery. This is actually a good problem to have—it means the starter is very active and vigorous! The yeast created simply needs a bit more food (flour) than what it's been given. When this happens, add the requisite 1 tablespoon of water, and 1 tablespoon, plus *1 teaspoon* flour. This little bit of extra flour will thicken the paste substantially, and calm the alcohol aroma. You can return to regular feedings the next day.

Sourdough Sponge

EVEN THOUGH THE SPONGE DOES NOT RISE MUCH, I RECOMMEND USING A BOWL LARGE ENOUGH TO HOLD the additional ingredients for the rest of the recipe. This not only saves you from doing extra washing up, but it also ensures that you are able to use every last bit of sponge as you add extra ingredients to make the dough.

When making the sourdough sponge, use 1 tablespoon of starter in the recipe, and then feed the rest of the starter in the pint jar with an additional tablespoon of flour and of water.

I tablespoon sourdough starter
⅓ cup (1⅔ ounces) all-purpose flour
¼ cup non-chlorinated water

In a large bowl, add the tablespoon of starter, flour, and water. Stir to thoroughly combine. Cover the bowl, setting it on a counter with a fairly warm, even temperature, and leave it for approximately 24 hours.

The mixture will be somewhat stiff as it is mixed. The next day, it will have loosened substantially, bubbles will have appeared, and the sponge will stretch if it's stirred. This means that the glutens have developed overnight.

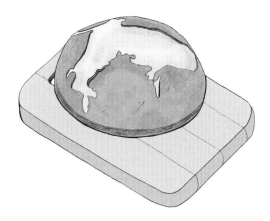

Sourdough Round

WHEN JIM LAHEY PUBLISHED HIS RECIPE FOR NO-KNEAD BREAD IN *THE NEW YORK TIMES* IN 2006, IT revolutionized how the home baker bakes bread in this country. The long proofing, almost no kneading, convection baking, and the use of a Dutch oven during baking to simulate steam seemed to be a modern solution to the age-old problem of obtaining a truly crusty loaf of bread in your home oven. But perhaps Mr. Lahey looked to the past for clues in writing his recipe.

Americans began hearthside cooking, or cooking and baking in cast-iron, lidded pots over the open hearths in their homes, as early as the eighteenth and nineteenth centuries. Of course, the method was different. While settlers preheated their Dutch ovens before adding the dough to bake, they often added hot trivets or coals to the pot to maintain a high temperature. Bread was a prized art. Commercial yeast was not even made available to the home baker until the mid-1800s, so not only did cooks bake beautiful loaves of bread daily, but they also created and maintained the yeast for those loaves. Kind of like what you're doing with your jar of sourdough!

Using a Dutch oven to bake is the simplest way of having a crackly, crunchy crust and a moist, bubbly interior. By dropping the dough into a hot pot and covering it quickly, you will trap any steam that will erupt during the baking process. This steam is what creates a firm crust. Other recipes have tried to solve the steam-creation problem by spritzing the entire oven with water, pouring boiling water into a heated pan, or throwing a few ice cubes onto the bottom of the stove. I've tried all of these techniques, and baking bread in a Dutch oven proves to be easy, reliable, and makes a beautiful loaf! It's not necessary to slash the dough prior to baking. You will be baking in a screaming hot pot, letting the dough fall where it may. It's more important to get the dough in the oven quickly and efficiently than it is to have a perfectly slashed loaf.

I like cast-iron Dutch ovens, but enamel ones will work well, too. The heft of cast-iron can be a bit cumbersome, but it holds heat remarkably well. Since you will be preheating the Dutch oven for a half hour at a high temperature (450°F), it is possible that the pot will become dark and dappled if you are using an enamel pot. So I recommend having a "bread pot" to bake with, or simply using cast-iron, which will not show dark smudges.

Makes 1 round

1 recipe Sourdough Sponge (page 70)
3½ scant cups (1 pound 1 ounce) all-purpose flour
⅓ cup (2 ounces) dark rye flour
1½ cups water, at room temperature
2 teaspoons kosher salt

In a large bowl, mix the sponge, all-purpose flour, rye flour, and water. Stir with a wooden spoon or rubber spatula until mixed. It is fine if the mixture is too stiff to become fully combined at this stage. Cover the bowl with plastic wrap and let rest for 20 minutes. This is an important stage; it allows the flours to fully absorb the water.

After 20 minutes have passed, you will notice that the flour is incorporated and hydrated. Using a pastry scraper, scrape the dough out onto a floured work surface. Sprinkle salt onto the dough, lightly wet your hands, and begin to knead the salt into the dough. If the dough becomes too sticky at any point, re-flour the work surface and re-moisten your hands. Having your hands slightly damp will make the dough less sticky to the touch. Because the proofing time is so lengthy, adding too much liquid is not a concern. As you continue to knead, the dough will become supple and more cohesive. When the salt has been thoroughly incorporated, about 3 minutes, return the dough to the bowl, cover, and let proof for approximately 24 hours.

The next day, the dough will have risen substantially, and the surface will be covered in large bubbles. Scrape the dough out onto a well-floured work surface. This time, with well-floured hands, begin kneading the dough softly, releasing the large air bubbles, and working the dough into a round (pages 22–23). Flour the work surface again, and place the round, seam-side down, onto the surface. Cover the round gently with a tea towel or light kitchen cloth. Let it rise for 1 hour.

Thirty minutes before baking, place an oven rack in the bottom third of the oven. Place a lidded Dutch oven in the center of the rack, and preheat to 450°F for 30 minutes.

Remove the Dutch oven from the oven; it will be very hot. Take the lid off; some smoke may have been trapped underneath. Gently slide your hand beneath the dough and drop it, seam-side down, into the pot. Place the lid on top of the pan, and put it in the oven. Bake for 30 minutes, covered. Remove the lid, and bake an additional 15 to 20 minutes. The loaf will be golden brown, quite firm, and sound hollow when tapped.

Immediately remove the bread from the Dutch oven with a spatula, and place it on a rack to cool to room temperature before enjoying. The bread may whine and crackle as it cools. You will notice also that the bread will turn from hard to sliceable as it cools.

WHY ADD RYE?

When making a standard sourdough round or loaf, you'll notice the addition of a small amount of rye flour. This is because whole grain flours ferment faster than all-purpose flour. This little bit of rye is higher in nutrients and sugars that the natural yeast can feed on. In these cases, whole wheat flour can be used in exchange for the rye flour. Although not exclusively necessary, the rye flour will ensure an adequate rise and a full-bodied structure in whichever type of bread you are baking. The amount is so minimal, the bread will still be considered a white bread, not a whole grain bread.

Sourdough Loaf

THERE ARE TIMES WHEN A ROUND JUST WON'T DO. YOU NEED THE EASY SLICEABLITY OF A LOAF, BUT still desire the tang of sourdough bread when you're making a BLT or having a slice of buttery toast. A sourdough loaf can be easily made using the very same recipe as the sourdough round. You will find that this loaf has a tighter crumb than the round; it is also lighter in color, with a more delicate crust. This recipe makes one abundant loaf. Take note that the second rise is very brief—only as long as it takes to preheat the oven. The bread will do a majority of its rising in the oven. Once extracted from the pan and cooled, this loaf is ready to be sliced and awaits your sandwich-fixings.

Makes 1 loaf

1 recipe Sourdough Round (page 71)

Follow both the ingredients and the directions for the sourdough round through the 24-hour rise.

Coat a standard loaf pan with cooking spray.

Using a pastry scraper, scrape the dough out onto a well-floured work surface. With well-floured hands, begin kneading the dough softly, releasing the large air bubbles. Form the dough into a loaf (page 20). Gently pick the dough up and place it into the pan, seam-side down.

Preheat the oven to 400°F for 15 minutes.

Place the loaf on the center rack of the oven, and bake for approximately 1 hour. The loaf will be light brown, and the top of the bread will have risen substantially while baking.

Immediately remove the bread from the pan. This may require slipping an off-set spatula around the perimeter of the pan. Once the loaf is released, cool to room temperature before slicing.

Whole Wheat Sourdough

ONCE YOU HAVE A SPONGE THAT YOU ARE SATISFIED WITH (AND I'M ASSUMING THAT NOW YOU DO!), there are numerous breads that you can bake. Use different flours, experiment with the their proportions, add seeds, nuts, or fruits—the possibilities are endless— it just requires practice and confidence. This recipe is for a basic whole wheat sourdough. Darker and coarser than the standard sourdough, this bread has the full-bodied flavor of a whole wheat sandwich bread, but the tang of a sourdough loaf. I've adorned this bread with some wheat germ, an ingredient I always keep in my refrigerator for sprucing up my breads. Its nutty flavor and nubby texture is satisfying, and it adds a wholesome, pleasing look to the bread that comes out of your oven.

Makes 1 round or loaf

1 recipe Sourdough Sponge (page 70)

2 cups (10 ounces) all-purpose flour

1¾ cups (just shy of 8 ounces)
whole wheat flour

1½ cups water, at room temperature

2½ teaspoons kosher salt

1½ teaspoons wheat germ

In a large bowl, mix the sponge, all-purpose flour, whole wheat flour, and water. Stir with a wooden spoon or rubber spatula until mixed. It is fine if the mixture is too stiff to become fully combined at this stage. Cover the bowl with plastic wrap and let rest for 20 minutes. This is an important stage; it allows the flours to fully absorb the water.

After 20 minutes have passed, you will notice that the flour is incorporated and hydrated. Using a pastry scraper, scrape the dough out onto a floured work surface. Sprinkle salt onto the dough, lightly wet your hands, and begin to knead the salt into the dough. If dough becomes too sticky at any point, re-flour the work surface and re-moisten your hands. Having your hands slightly damp will make the dough less sticky to the touch. Because the proofing time is so lengthy, adding too much liquid is not a concern. As you continue to knead, the dough will become supple and more cohesive. When the salt has been thoroughly incorporated, about 3 minutes, return the dough to the bowl, cover, and let proof for approximately 24 hours.

The next day, the dough will have risen substantially, and the surface will be covered in large bubbles. Scrape the dough out onto a well-floured work surface. This time, with well-floured hands, begin kneading the dough softly, releasing the large air bubbles, and working the dough into a round or a loaf (pages 20–23).

TO BAKE A ROUND: Flour the work surface again, and place the round, seam-side down, onto the surface. Cover gently with a tea towel or light kitchen cloth. Let it rise for 1 hour. Before baking, brush the surface of the dough with water, and sprinkle on the wheat germ.

Thirty minutes before baking, place an oven rack in the bottom third of the oven. Place a lidded Dutch oven in the center of the rack, and preheat to 450°F for 30 minutes.

Remove the Dutch oven from the oven; it will be very hot. Take the lid off; some smoke may have been trapped under it. Gently slide your hand beneath the dough, and drop it, seam-side down, into the pot. Place the lid on top of the pan, and put it in the oven. Bake for 30 minutes, covered. Remove the lid and bake an additional 15 to 20 minutes. The loaf will be golden brown, quite firm, and sound hollow when tapped.

Immediately remove the bread from the Dutch oven with a spatula, and place on a rack to cool to room temperature before enjoying. The bread may whine and crackle as it cools. You will notice also that the bread will turn from hard to sliceable as it cools.

TO BAKE A LOAF: Gently place the loaf in a greased loaf pan, and preheat the oven to 400°F for 15 minutes. Before baking, brush the surface of the dough with water, and sprinkle on the wheat germ.

Place the loaf on the center rack of the oven, and bake for about 1 hour. The loaf will be light brown, and the top of the bread will have risen substantially while baking.

Immediately remove the bread from the pan. This may require slipping an off-set spatula around the perimeter of the pan. Once the loaf is released, cool to room temperature before slicing.

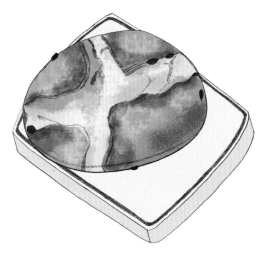

Sourdough Rye Raisin-Walnut Loaf

IN THE WORLD OF FLOUR, RYE IS ALMOST A SPECIES UNTO ITSELF. ONCE THE FLOUR OF PEASANTS, RYE is hospitable to growth even in poor soil and frigid climates. The flour creates wonderful breads—rich, dark, wholesome, and nutty. Rye is similar in taste to whole wheat breads (many people incorrectly assume rye is just another whole *wheat* bread), but it is unique unto itself. Rye flour does not contain the same gluten-producing structure as wheat flour, meaning rye breads will not be as chewy as pure wheat breads. Rye is an extremely healthy flour, containing extra bran and minerals, but this heft leads to lower rise. In this country, most of the rye breads that we eat include wheat flour as well. In essence, they are wheat breads flavored with rye flour. By baking this way, you still get all of the delicious, rustic qualities of a rye bread, while having the ease of baking a wheat bread.

This loaf has the ideal proportions of rye and wheat flours. The sourdough starter adds a bit of tang, playing off the sweet raisins and the earthy walnuts. This is a coarser loaf of bread with a slightly dense interior, but it has a crisp and chewy crust. I love this bread toasted in the morning with some salted butter. But I always save a few slices to make croutons out of, too. They are perfect tossed in a salad with some dark, peppery greens.

Makes 1 round

1 recipe Sourdough Sponge (page 70)
2¼ cups (11¼ ounces) all-purpose flour
1 cup (5 ounces) dark rye flour
1⅓ cups water, at room temperature
2 teaspoons kosher salt
½ cup (2¾ ounces) raisins
½ cup (2 ounces) walnuts, coarsely chopped

In a large bowl, mix the sponge, all-purpose flour, rye flour, and water. Stir with a wooden spoon or rubber spatula until mixed. It is fine if the mixture is too stiff to become fully combined at this stage. Cover and let rest for 20 minutes. This is an important stage. It allows the flours to fully absorb the water.

After 20 minutes have passed, you will notice that the flour is incorporated and hydrated. Using a pastry scraper, scrape the dough out onto a floured work surface. Sprinkle half of the salt onto the dough, lightly wet your hands, and begin to knead the salt into the dough. If the dough becomes too sticky at any point, re-flour the work surface and re-moisten your hands. Having your hands slightly damp will make the dough less sticky to the touch. Because the proofing time is so lengthy, adding too much liquid is not a concern.

As the ingredients begin to become incorporated, add the rest of the salt and half of the raisins and walnuts, and continue to knead. Add the rest of the raisins and the walnuts to the dough, and complete the kneading process. As you continue to knead, the dough will become supple and more cohesive. When everything has been thoroughly incorporated, about 3 to 5 minutes, return the dough to the bowl, cover, and let proof for approximately 24 hours.

The next day, the dough will have risen substantially, and the surface will be covered in large bubbles. Scrape the dough out onto a well-floured work surface. This time, with well-floured hands, begin kneading the dough softly, releasing the large air bubbles, and working the dough into a round (pages 22–23).

Flour the work surface again, and place the round, seam-side down, onto the surface. Cover gently with a tea towel or light kitchen cloth. Let it rise for 1 hour.

Thirty minutes before baking, place an oven rack in the bottom third of the oven. Place a lidded Dutch oven in the center of the rack, and preheat to 450°F for 30 minutes.

Remove the Dutch oven from the oven; it will be very hot. Take the lid off; some smoke may have been trapped under it. Gently slide your hand underneath the dough and drop it, seam-side down, into the pot. Place the lid on top of the pan, and put it in the oven. Bake for 30 minutes, covered. Remove the lid, and bake an additional 10 to 15 minutes. The loaf will be golden brown, be quite firm, and sound hollow when tapped.

Immediately remove the bread from the Dutch oven with a spatula, and place it on a rack to cool to room temperature before enjoying. The bread may whine and crackle as it cools. You will notice also that the bread will turn from hard to sliceable as it cools.

Sourdough Cranberry Bread

CRANBERRIES DON'T HAVE TO BE RELEGATED TO THE THANKSGIVING TABLE! THIS TART BERRY IS ONE of the true New World fruits, and it still flourishes up and down the coast of New England. But have no fear—this recipe uses the dried sort, so feel free to enjoy this loaf any time of year, no matter where you live. This bread is a standout with the sour punch of the cranberries and the tanginess of the bread. It also utilizes wheat germ, giving the loaf a toasty, earthy flavor. The berries impart a rosy cast to the bread, and baked with both whole wheat and all-purpose flour, this bread is beautiful and sustaining.

Makes 1 round

I recipe Sourdough Sponge (page 70)

2 cups (10 ounces) all-purpose flour

1¼ cups (6¼ ounces) whole wheat flour

¼ cup (I ounce) wheat germ

1⅓ cups water, at room temperature

2¼ teaspoons kosher salt

½ cup (2¼ ounces) dried cranberries

In a large bowl, mix the sponge, all-purpose flour, whole wheat flour, wheat germ, and water. Stir with a wooden spoon or rubber spatula until mixed. It is fine if the mixture is too stiff to become fully combined at this stage. Cover the bowl with plastic wrap and let rest for 20 minutes. This is an important stage; it allows the flours to fully absorb the water.

After 20 minutes have passed, you will notice that the flour is incorporated and hydrated. Using a pastry scraper, scrape the dough out onto a floured work surface. Sprinkle half of the salt onto the dough, lightly wet your hands, and begin to knead the salt into the dough. If the dough becomes too sticky at any point, re-flour the work surface and re-moisten your hands. Having your hands slightly damp will make the dough less sticky to the touch. Because the proofing time is so lengthy, adding too much liquid is not a concern.

As the ingredients begin to become incorporated, add the rest of the salt and half of the cranberries, continuing to knead. Add the rest of the cranberries to the dough, and complete the kneading process. As you do so, the dough will become supple and more cohesive. When everything has been thoroughly incorporated, about 3 to 5 minutes, return the dough to the bowl, cover, and let proof for approximately 24 hours.

The next day, the dough will have risen substantially, and the surface will be covered in large bubbles. Scrape the dough out onto a well-floured work surface. This time, with well-floured hands, begin kneading the dough softly, releasing the large air bubbles, and working the dough into a round (pages 22–23).

Flour the work surface again, and place the round, seam-side down, onto the surface. Cover gently with a tea towel or light kitchen cloth. Let it rise for 1 hour.

Thirty minutes before baking, place the oven rack in the bottom third of the oven. Place a lidded Dutch oven in the center of the rack, and preheat to 450°F for 30 minutes.

Remove the Dutch oven from the oven; it will be very hot. Take the lid off; some smoke may have been trapped under it. Gently slide your hand underneath the dough, and drop it, seam-side down, into the pot. Place the lid on top of the pan, and put it in the oven. Bake for 30 minutes, covered. Remove the lid, and bake an additional 10 to 15 minutes. The loaf will be golden brown, be quite firm, and sound hollow when tapped.

Immediately remove the bread from the Dutch oven with a spatula, and place it on a rack to cool to room temperature before enjoying. The bread may whine and crackle as it cools. You will notice also that the bread will turn from hard to sliceable as it cools.

ROLLS

BREAD COMES IN A VARIETY OF SHAPES AND SIZES. SOMETIMES A LOAF IS not optimal. In those cases, we turn to the roll. Rolls have a venerable tradition abroad, but American bread bakers have created new specialties as well as placed their mark on old-world creations—from the buttery Parker House roll (page 88) of Boston to the bagels (page 102) of the Jewish ghettos in the Lower East Side of Manhattan. Perhaps it's because a roll can be eaten in so many ways. Whether sopping up gravy during dinnertime, sliced in half for making sandwiches, or humbly sitting beside a morning cup of coffee, these diminutive breads have been gobbled up by Americans with gusto. In this chapter, you will find rolls unique unto themselves, as well as a Master Roll recipe (page 85), which shows various shaping and encrusting techniques. With this information at hand, you may just find your next go-to, self-contained favorite.

SHAPING A ROLL

In this chapter, I have isolated a few exemplary rolls, but almost any bread that is intended to be a loaf can be a roll—and vice versa. It is the shape that creates this type of bread. While dough can simply be divided and baked, there is a particular shaping method that creates smooth, tight rounds.

After your dough has been divided—either by weight, using a scale, or the less exact method, by sight—place one piece of dough on the work surface. Notice I did not say "well-floured." As counterintuitive as it is to the acquired knowledge of your bread baking experiences, shaping a roll doesn't require an abundance of flour. You want the work surface clean and dry, although you may appreciate your hands to be floured *lightly*. During the shaping process, you want friction to be created between the work surface and the dough; this will help to create a tight ball.

Since you are making rolls, which by definition are small, shaping can and should be done using one hand. Cup your hand over the mound of dough, like a cage. With the sides of your thumb and pinky finger planted firmly on the work surface, begin to glide your hand and the dough around in a circle[19]. This motion is quick. The dough may be sticky and uncooperative at first, but as you continue the process, the dough will begin to take shape. As your hand circles, the dough will nudge against the outside fingers, which helps the dough to retain its shape. It will begin to perk up, a tight skin will begin to develop, and the crest of the roll will soon meet the palm of your hand. The entire process takes no more than 30 seconds to complete.

Once roll is formed, gently pick it up and place it on a baking pan. The dough will be fairly delicate, but the shape will hold. What once was misshapen will now be smooth. It will continue to rise in this shape, and you will soon have warm rolls to dot with butter or enjoy with a meal.

Master Roll Recipe

WHAT WOULD THANKSGIVING BE WITHOUT A BUTTERY ROLL TO GO ALONGSIDE YOUR TURKEY AND gravy? Or how about a pillow-soft roll sliced in two for the bread in your weekday sandwich? Slathered with jam and an extra pat of butter, then eaten on the go as you dash out the door on your way to work—a good roll can be all of those things. Once you have mastered the basics, this roll recipe will prove invaluable. If a petite side roll is what you desire, you can easily scale down the size of the individual rolls that you make. Want something more substantial? Alter the proportions.

This roll is soft, buttery, and infinitely malleable. Following you will find several recipes that all use this master recipe with different, delicious results, but the basic is a delight all on its own.

Makes 18 rolls

¼ cup warm water (100° to 115°F)

2¼ teaspoons (1 package) dry yeast

Pinch of sugar

1 egg

1 cup whole milk, at room temperature

4 tablespoons (2 ounces) unsalted butter, at room temperature

2 tablespoons sugar

2 teaspoons kosher salt

3¼ to 3¾ cups (1 pound, ¼ ounce to 1 pound, 2¾ ounces)
all-purpose flour

In the bowl of a stand mixer, mix the water, yeast, and sugar together. Allow the mixture to bloom. It should become bubbly and smell yeasty, about 10 minutes.

In the same bowl, fitted with the paddle attachment, add the egg, milk, butter, sugar, salt, and 3 cups (15 ounces) of the flour. Mix briefly at low speed until the mixture becomes web-like and dough begins to cling to the paddle.

Remove the paddle and attach the dough hook. With the mixer on low speed, begin kneading with the dough hook and adding additional flour by the spoonful. The dough will become a more cohesive mass, more elastic, and start to pull away from the sides of the bowl. It is important to watch the dough during this process. All of the flour should be incorporated at each step, but you don't want the dough to become too dry or heavy. Stop the mixer intermittently and touch the dough; it should still be tacky, but not too sticky. The dough will take anywhere from $\frac{1}{4}$ to $\frac{3}{4}$ cup ($1\frac{1}{4}$ to $3\frac{3}{4}$ ounces of additional flour). It should be smooth and free of lumps. This kneading process will take 6 to 10 minutes.

Empty the dough out onto a well-floured surface, scrape the bowl with a pastry scraper, adding any bits of dough from the bowl to the mound, and gently knead it into a ball. Put it back into the bowl, and place a piece of plastic wrap on the surface of the dough.

Place it in a warm spot, and let it rise for approximately $1\frac{1}{2}$ hours, or until doubled in bulk.

Pull back the plastic wrap, and empty the dough out onto a well-floured surface. Fold the dough over, once in each direction, to release the gases. The dough will weigh about 2 pounds. Divide it into 18 equally-sized pieces, weighing approximately $1\frac{1}{2}$ ounces each. Form each mound of dough into a roll shape (page 83). Place them on a parchment paper-lined baking tray.

Cover with a tea towel or light kitchen cloth, and let the rolls rise for about 1 hour, or until almost doubled in bulk.

Move the oven rack in the middle of the oven. Fifteen minutes prior to baking, preheat to 400°F, and remove the tea towel from the tray.

Bake for 15 to 18 minutes, or until the tops of the rolls are golden brown. Remove the rolls from the oven, and set the pan on a cooling rack for approximately 5 minutes. Take the rolls off the pan, return them to the rack, and allow them to cool until just warm or room temperature.

Cloverleaf Rolls

HERE IS ANOTHER WAY TO MAKE THE MASTER ROLL RECIPE. THESE FESTIVE, SELF-CONTAINED ROLLS are baked in a standard muffin tin, perfect for holiday dinners. Each roll is actually three in one. During the second rise and the baking process, they bake into a cloverleaf shape, and then can be pulled apart. Buttery and soft, these rolls are best fresh from the oven.

Makes 12 rolls

1 recipe Master Roll (page 85)
1 tablespoon (½ ounce) unsalted butter, melted

Follow the Master Roll recipe through the first rise. With a pastry brush, paint the melted butter in each one of the cups of a standard muffin tin.

Pull back the plastic wrap, and empty the dough out onto a well-floured surface. Fold the dough over, once in each direction, to release the gases. The dough will weigh about 2 pounds. Divide it into 3 equally sized, large portions. Then further divide each portion into 12 pieces, weighing about ⅞ ounce each. Working with one piece at a time, form each into a roll shape (page 83). At completion, you should have 36 small, spherical pieces. Into each cup of the muffin tin, place 3 pieces of dough. Continue filling the cups until the tin is full. It is fine if the pieces have to be nestled snugly in the muffin cups.

Cover with a tea towel or light kitchen cloth, and let the rolls rise for 45 minutes to 1 hour, or until almost doubled in bulk.

Arrange the oven rack in the middle of the oven. Fifteen minutes prior to baking, preheat to 375°F, and remove the tea towel from the tin.

Bake for 20 to 22 minutes, or until the tops of the rolls are golden brown. Enjoy while still warm. Any leftovers can be frozen. Simply thaw at room temperature, and then reheat at 300°F for about 5 minutes.

Parker House Rolls

THESE ADDICTIVE ROLLS ARE A TRUE NEW ENGLAND SPECIALTY, AND AS WITH ANY BIT OF CULINARY lore, there is a charming, though possibly apocryphal, story behind them. During the 1870s, The Parker House was a grand hotel in downtown Boston that employed a temperamental pastry chef. This chef became disgruntled with a guest at the hotel, threw an unfinished batch of rolls into the oven, and stormed off. Instead of destroying the breads that he was baking, moments later, he pulled the rolls from the oven and saw that each now had a crease like a clamshell on them. As it turned out, the crease was the perfect vehicle for a generous slathering of butter. The rolls were a hit and became a regular at the Parker House, where they are still served today. Over time, these rolls became quite the rage and began appearing in cookbooks such as the *Boston Cooking-School Cook Book* in the late nineteenth century.

Today you can find countless recipes for Parker House Rolls. You will read many recipes that coat these rolls in melted butter prior to baking. I am all for a buttery roll, but I have found that this application makes it difficult for these rolls to maintain the emblematic fold that makes a Parker House Roll. Instead, I have chosen to insert a knob of cold butter, and then fold each roll around the butter. The butter melts upon baking, and the pocket stays intact. Problem solved with a buttery solution.

Makes 16 rolls

I recipe Master Roll (page 85), using only 2 tablespoons
(I ounce) room temperature butter in the dough
2 tablespoons (I ounce) unsalted butter, chilled, cut into 16 squares
I tablespoon (½ ounce) unsalted butter, melted

Follow the Master Roll recipe, incorporating only 2 tablespoons of butter into the dough, through the first rise.

Pull back the plastic wrap, and empty the dough out onto a well-floured surface. Fold the dough over, once in each direction, to release the gases. The dough will weigh about 2 pounds. Divide it into 16 equally-sized pieces, weighing approximately 2 ounces each. Working with one piece of dough at a time, form each mound of dough into a roll shape (page 83). Lightly flour the top of the dough, and then roll it out to into an oval or circular shape, approximately 3 inches in diameter.

With the back of a dinner knife, make an indentation in the center of the dough. Place one piece of chilled butter on one side of the indentation, and then fold in two, gently pressing the two sides together. The fold should be slightly askew, showing the two halves of the circle. Place on a parchment paper-lined baking tray, and repeat with remaining portions of dough. Brush the rolls with 1 tablespoon of melted butter.

Cover the rolls with a tea towel or light kitchen cloth, and let the rolls rise for approximately 45 minutes, or until almost doubled in bulk.

Arrange the oven rack in the middle of the oven. Fifteen minutes prior to baking, preheat to 400°F, and remove the tea towel from the tray.

Bake for 13 to 15 minutes, or until the tops of the rolls are golden brown. Enjoy while still warm. Any leftovers can be frozen. Simply thaw at room temperature, and then reheat at 300°F for about 5 minutes.

Dutch Crunch Rolls

IF YOU GREW UP IN THE SAN FRANCISCO BAY AREA, YOU WILL BE HAPPY TO HAVE FINALLY FOUND THE recipe on which you enjoyed many turkey sandwiches. If you grew up outside of Northern California, you probably will say, "What kind of roll?" or "I thought this was an American bread book. Why am I making a *Dutch* bread?" A soft and chewy roll, Dutch Crunch has a peculiar and tantalizing exterior—a shatteringly crisp, golden brown carapace. Contrasted with the soft interior, this regional specialty is an exercise in texture.

The recipe is an adaptation of a Dutch bread (hence the name) called *tijgerbrood*, or tiger bread, referring to the bread's mottled crust. When Galli's Sanitary Bakery, located just south of San Francisco in San Bruno, began making the bread over a century ago, it was an instant success. It turned out that customers had room in their hearts for more than just sourdough in the Bay Area, and soon other bakeries began supplying legions of diners with Dutch Crunch as well. It has been more than a century, but this bread's popularity has not waned; you can still find Dutch Crunch in nearly every delicatessen and grocery store in the Bay Area.

The topping is a mixture of yeast and white rice flour, which is applied during the second rise. (Make sure it's not sweetened rice flour. Unsweetened rice flour is getting easier to find due the preponderance of gluten-free flours in grocery stores nowadays.) This paste crackles when it's baked, leaving a golden exterior and a terrific texture.

These rolls make great sandwiches. When I was young, my standard would be turkey, sprouts, and mustard on Dutch Crunch, and I still love it. But if sprouts are too "California" for you, top these rolls with whatever suits your fancy!

Makes 12 rolls

I recipe Master Roll (page 85)

DUTCH CRUNCH TOPPING:

4½ teaspoons (2 packages) dry yeast

I tablespoon sugar

¼ teaspoon kosher salt

⅓ cup (2 ounces) unsweetened white rice flour

I teaspoon vegetable oil

⅓ cup warm water (100° to 115°F)

Follow the Master Roll recipe to the first rise. Cover with plastic wrap on the surface of the dough, and allow the rolls to rise partially, for about 1 hour, and then make the topping.

In a medium-size bowl, whisk the yeast, sugar, salt, and rice flour together until combined. Add the oil and the water, and continue to whisk until well-incorporated. The mixture should be smooth and free of lumps. It should have a paste-like consistency. Allow it to rise until bread is finished proofing, about one half hour.

Pull back the plastic wrap, and empty the dough out onto a well-floured surface. Fold the dough over, once in each direction, to release the gases. The dough will weigh about 2 pounds. Divide into 12 equally-sized pieces, weighing approximately $2\frac{1}{2}$ ounces each. Form each mound of dough into a roll shape (pages 83–84). Place them on a parchment paper-lined baking tray.

The topping will have risen substantially. With a spoon, stir the mixture down. Spoon the topping onto the rolls, letting it drip down the sides. The topping should not only cover the tops of the rolls, but the sides as well. There will be just enough topping to completely cover the rolls. Let them rise uncovered for about 1 hour, or until almost doubled in bulk.

Arrange the oven rack in the middle of the oven, and fifteen minutes prior to baking, preheat to 375°F.

Bake for 22 to 25 minutes, or until the rolls are crackly and golden brown. Remove the rolls from the oven, and set the pan on a cooling rack for approximately 5 minutes. Take the rolls off the pan, return them to the rack, and allow them to cool to room temperature.

Cheddar Snails

GROWING UP, THERE WAS A BAKERY IN THE MALL (NO, NOT A QUAINT MAIN STREET, THIS WAS THE suburbs) that made the most delicious cheese bread. Or at least it was delicious to my eight-year-old palate. The bread itself was nothing special, and the cheese was hardly top-of-the-line, but together, this cheese bread was sublime. The cheese melted into the bread, creating pockets of savory flavor. It was bubbly, and upon cooling, the cheese became chewy, crispy, and even more tantalizing. As you can see, this cheese bread was culinary perfection to a child's stomach.

This recipe uses the Master Roll recipe. Buttery and light, it already leaves the mall cheese bread behind in terms of bread quality. I have opted to use a sharp cheddar cheese; I wanted the pungency. There is also a bit of freshly ground black pepper both in the dough and sprinkled on top of the rolls; this plays well off the salty cheese. But the most important addendum is the shape of these rolls. Work the dough into a rectangle (as if you were making cinnamon rolls), sprinkle on the cheese, and then roll and slice the dough. Upon baking, the cheese melts within the snail, and some oozes out on top of the roll, getting brown and crisp—truly delectable. Once you pull these snails from the oven, that mall bread (if you too remember it fondly) will become a distant memory.

Makes 12 to 14 rolls

I recipe Master Roll, minus the I tablespoon sugar (page 85)

¼ teaspoon freshly ground black pepper,
plus additional for sprinkling on top of the snails

2 tablespoons coarse cornmeal

1½ cups (6 ounces) sharp cheddar cheese, grated

I egg

Follow the Master Roll recipe, omitting the tablespoon of sugar and adding in $\frac{1}{4}$ teaspoon pepper, through the first rise.

Sprinkle cornmeal evenly onto a large baking sheet. Set aside.

Pull back the plastic wrap, and empty the dough out onto a well-floured surface. Fold the dough over, once in each direction, to release the gases. Roll the dough out to approximately 16 x 10 inches. Sprinkle the cheese over the dough, leaving a $\frac{1}{2}$ inch of space on the longer sides of the dough. Press the cheese lightly into the dough. Roll it tightly to form a cylinder 16 inches long. Pinch the final seam of dough to the cylinder, closing the roll. Gently roll the cylinder back and forth to make sure that it is amply secure and moves easily from the counter.

With a sharp knife or pastry cutter, cut the dough into 12 or 14 equal pieces, a little over 1 inch in length. Place each snail onto the pan, leaving a bit of room between each roll. It is fine if the rolls bake together somewhat.

Cover with a tea towel or light kitchen cloth, and let them rise for approximately 1 hour, or until almost doubled in bulk.

Arrange the oven rack in the middle of the oven. Fifteen minutes prior to baking, preheat to 350°F, and remove the tea towel from the pan.

In a small bowl, mix the egg and 1 tablespoon water together. Brush the egg wash onto the snails, then sprinkle them with additional pepper.

Bake for 20 to 25 minutes, or until the tops of the rolls are golden brown and cheese is bubbling outside the rolls. Remove the snails from the oven, and set the pan on a cooling rack for approximately 5 minutes. Take the snails off the pan, return them to the rack, and allow them to cool until just warm or room temperature.

Pumpkin Rosemary Rolls

THE PUMPKIN IS ONE OF THE INDIGENOUS FOODS OF AMERICA. ROASTED OR BAKED, SETTLERS IN THE New World found this novel ingredient similar to the hardy winter squashes that they had cooked with in Europe. They adapted the pumpkin into unique recipes from pies to purées, and of course, bread—but *this* bread is not the much-loved Halloween-time quickbread, spiced and baked in a loaf pan. This recipe is for a buttery dinner roll, tinged orange with pumpkin purée, scented with woodsy rosemary, and finally, sprinkled with coarse salt. One taste of these rolls, and I promise, you won't be missing the sweetness or the classic spices of that October quickbread. These may become a new holiday tradition!

Makes 18 rolls

¼ cup warm water (100° to 115°F)

4 teaspoons dry yeast

Pinch of sugar

1 cup (9½ ounces) canned pumpkin

2 eggs

4 tablespoons (2 ounces) unsalted butter, at room temperature,
plus 2 tablespoons (1 ounce) unsalted butter,
divided and melted

¼ cup (1¾ ounces) sugar

1½ teaspoons kosher salt

2 teaspoons fresh rosemary, finely diced

3 to 4 cups (15 ounces to 1 pound, 1½ ounces)
all-purpose flour

½ teaspoon coarse salt, such as Maldon,
or flaked sea salt

In a small bowl or glass, mix the water, yeast, and sugar together. Allow the mixture to bloom. It should become bubbly and smell yeasty, about 10 minutes.

In the bowl of a stand mixer fitted with the paddle attachment, add the pumpkin, eggs, 4 tablespoons (2 ounces) butter, sugar, salt, rosemary, and 2½ cups (12½ ounces) of flour.

At low speed, mix until just combined. Add the yeast mixture, and mix briefly. The mixture will become web-like and more difficult to mix with the paddle attachment.

Remove the paddle and attach the dough hook. With the mixer on low speed, begin kneading with the dough hook, adding additional flour in $1/4$- to $1/2$-cup increments. The dough will become a more cohesive mass, more elastic, and start to pull away from the sides of the bowl. It is important to watch the dough during this process. All of the flour should be incorporated at each step, but you don't want the dough to become too dry or heavy. Stop the mixer intermittently and touch the dough; it should still be tacky, but not too sticky. The dough will take anywhere from $1/2$ cup to 1 cup ($2^1/_2$ to 5 ounces) of additional flour. It should be smooth and free of lumps. This kneading process will take 6 to 10 minutes.

Empty the dough out onto a well-floured surface, scrape the bowl with a pastry scraper, adding any bits of dough from the bowl to the mound, and gently knead it into a ball. Put it back into the bowl, and place a piece of plastic wrap on the surface of the dough.

Place it in a warm spot, and let it rise $1^1/_2$ to 2 hours, or until doubled in bulk.

Grease a 13 x 9-inch pan with 1 tablespoon of melted butter, and set aside.

Pull back the plastic wrap, and empty the dough out onto a well-floured surface. Fold the dough over, once in each direction, to release the gases. Divide the dough into 18 equally-sized pieces. Form each mound of dough into a roll shape (pages 83–84). Place in the prepared pan.

Cover the pan with plastic wrap, and let the rolls rise for 1 to $1^1/_2$ hours, or until doubled in bulk.

Arrange the oven rack in the middle of the oven, and fifteen minutes prior to baking, preheat to 375°F.

Remove the plastic wrap. Brush the surface of the rolls with the remaining tablespoon of melted butter, and then sprinkle with salt.

Bake for 20 to 25 minutes, or until golden brown. Enjoy while still warm.

Cornmeal Rolls

FOR FEEDING LIVESTOCK AND FEEDING PEOPLE, IN KANSAS THEY GROW CORN! THE EASTERN PORTION of the state is considered part of America's Corn Belt, and naturally, cornmeal is a wholesome by-product of this production. Of course, you can bake a cornbread with this meal (I have a few recipes for you starting on page 163), but in Kansas they also bake these delectable, yeasted cornmeal rolls.

Buttery and golden yellow from the cornmeal, these aren't the type of rolls that declare their corniness. It is merely a suggestion. Delicately sweet and wonderfully light, these rolls are just the thing to eat alongside your supper. Nestled in a cake pan, they plump upon baking and tear apart beautifully. The key to keeping these rolls light is not adding too much flour. Touch the dough often when kneading, and stop adding flour when the dough still has a bit of stickiness. A soft dough will make a light roll.

Makes 16 rolls

½ cup (2½ ounces) plus 1 tablespoon cornmeal

1 cup whole milk

½ cup warm water (100° to 115°F)

2¼ teaspoons (1 package) dry yeast

Pinch of sugar

1 egg

4 tablespoons (2 ounces) unsalted butter,
at room temperature, plus 2 tablespoons (1 ounce) unsalted butter,
divided and melted

¼ cup (1¾ ounces) sugar

2 teaspoons kosher salt

2½ to 3 cups (12½ to 15 ounces) all-purpose flour

In a medium-size saucepan, whisk the cornmeal and milk together. Over medium heat, whisking constantly, bring the mixture to a simmer. The cornmeal will absorb the liquid and become more difficult to stir. When the mixture has reached a porridge consistency, about 5 minutes, remove it from the heat. Cool until just warm.

In a small bowl or glass, mix the water, yeast, and sugar together. Allow the mixture to bloom. It should become bubbly and smell yeasty, about 10 minutes.

In the bowl of a stand mixer fitted with the paddle attachment, add the cornmeal paste, egg, 4 tablespoons (2 ounces) butter, sugar, salt, and 2 cups (10 ounces) of flour. Mix briefly at low speed, until the mixture becomes web-like and dough begins to cling to the paddle.

Remove the paddle and attach the dough hook. With the mixer on low speed, begin kneading with the dough hook, adding additional flour by the spoonful. The dough will become a more cohesive mass, more elastic, and start to pull away from the sides of the bowl. It is important to watch the dough during this process. All of the flour should be incorporated at each step, but you don't want the dough to become too dry or heavy. Stop the mixer intermittently and touch the dough; it should still be tacky, but not too sticky. The dough will take anywhere from $1/2$ to 1 cup ($2^1/_2$ to 5 ounces). It should be smooth and free of lumps. This kneading process will take 6 to 10 minutes.

Empty the dough out onto a well-floured surface, scrape the bowl with a pastry scraper, adding any bits of dough from the bowl to the mound, and gently knead it into a ball. Put it back into the bowl, and place a piece of plastic wrap on the surface of the dough.

Place it in a warm spot, and let it rise for approximately $1^1/_2$ hours, or until doubled in bulk.

Grease two 8- or 9-inch round cake pans with 1 tablespoon melted butter, and set them aside.

Pull back the plastic wrap, and empty the dough out onto a well-floured surface. Fold the dough over, once in each direction, to release the gases. The dough will weigh about 2 pounds. Divide into 16 equally-sized pieces, weighing approximately 2 ounces each. Form each round of dough into a roll shape (pages 83–84). Place each roll into the cake pans, 8 per pan, leaving a bit of room between the rolls. They will continue to rise.

Cover with a tea towel or light kitchen cloth, and let the rolls rise for about 1 hour, or until almost doubled in bulk.

Arrange the oven rack in the middle of the oven. Fifteen minutes prior to baking, preheat to 375°F, and remove the tea towel from the pans.

Brush the rolls with the remaining tablespoon of butter, and sprinkle with an additional tablespoon of cornmeal.

Bake for 18 to 23 minutes, or until the tops of the rolls are golden brown. Remove the rolls from the oven, and set them on a cooling rack for approximately 5 minutes. Enjoy the rolls while still warm.

Bride's Biscuits

IS THIS A BISCUIT, OR IS IT A ROLL? ACTUALLY, IT'S BOTH. GETTING LAYER UPON LAYER OF FLAKY, Southern-style biscuits can be a challenge. Reasons could be: The ingredients aren't cold enough, you're working the dough too much, or you're not working fast enough. If you have any one of these issues, the biscuits could turn out a sodden mess. Enter the Bride's Biscuit; these biscuits ensure a light, fluffy biscuit even if the inexcusable is done to them with the addition of yeast. Just a bit of yeast takes the pressure out of baking this staple. The biscuits are called Bride's Biscuits because even a newlywed, who may lack capability and confidence in the kitchen, can still bake a biscuit that's a mile high. (Sexist I know, but bear with me!) I think the addition of yeast makes these biscuits more substantial and more like a roll than a quickbread, while still remaining light. They're the perfect match for breakfast sandwiches, or for a sweet pairing, try macerated strawberries for shortcakes.

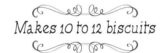

Makes 10 to 12 biscuits

¼ cup warm water (100° to 115°F)

1½ teaspoons dry yeast

Pinch of sugar

2½ cups (12½ ounces) all-purpose flour

1 teaspoon baking powder

½ teaspoon baking soda

1 tablespoon sugar

¾ teaspoon kosher salt

4 tablespoons (2 ounces) unsalted butter, chilled,
cut into ½-inch cubes, plus 1 tablespoon unsalted butter, melted

1 cup buttermilk

In a small bowl or glass, mix the water, yeast, and sugar together. Allow the mixture to bloom. It should become bubbly and smell yeasty, about 10 minutes.

In a medium-size bowl, whisk the flour, baking powder, baking soda, sugar, and salt together to blend. The mixture should be light and free of lumps.

Add the cubed butter and toss gently to coat in the flour mixture. With your fingertips, work the butter cubes into the flour mixture, rubbing the larger pieces of butter between your fingers until you have pea-size pieces.

Add the yeast mixture and buttermilk, all at once. With a wooden spoon or rubber spatula, mix until just blended and coming together to form a dough. The dough should not be too wet and will come together quite easily. Cover with plastic wrap, and place in the refrigerator to chill for 1 hour.

Arrange the oven rack in the middle of the oven. Fifteen minutes prior to baking, preheat the oven to 450°F.

Remove the plastic wrap, and empty the dough onto a clean, well-floured surface. Gently pat the dough out into a rectangle approximately 12 x 8 inches. Lightly flour the surface. Fold the dough into thirds, as if you are folding a letter. Scrape the folded dough from the work surface; if necessary, flour the surface again. Once more, pat the dough into a rectangle, flour lightly, and fold into thirds. Finally, pat the dough out to a thickness of approximately 3/4 inch.

With a well-floured 2- or 2 1/2-inch round biscuit cutter, cut the biscuits out, and place them on a baking sheet. You may reshape biscuits from the scraps, but they will not rise as high as the first cutting. Brush the tops of the biscuits with melted butter.

Bake for 12 to 15 minutes, or until the biscuits are a light, golden brown. Serve immediately. Biscuits are best eaten the same day as they are baked, but any leftovers can be eaten warm the next day. Simply reheat in a 300°F oven for 5 minutes.

Water-Proofed Rolls

IF YOU'RE LOOKING FOR THE MOST UNIQUE WAY TO PROOF A ROLL, LOOK NO FURTHER. IF YOU'RE LOOK-
ing for a little interesting dinner conversation, look no further. If you're looking for a light,
delicious, buttery roll, look no further. This recipe has it all covered. I've adapted it from *Beard
on Bread*, written by none other than American food pioneer James Beard. This funky relic
is filled with delectable recipes and entertaining anecdotes, but the most enthralling recipe
I found in it is for Water-Proofed Bread. I've done my research and have yet to find another
recipe for it. It reads like a basic, dairy-heavy dough recipe until instructions are given for the
first rise. You put the dough on a well-floured tea towel, wrap it loosely like a package, and
then submerge the package in warm water. Initially, the dough will sink, but about 45 minutes
later, the dough package will become billowy and bob to the surface of the water, meaning
your bread has risen substantially. Yes, it's true that this proofing method is a bit messy. As
you would guess, the dough gets quite wet and webby. But it holds together and makes the
lightest, most luxurious, *brioche*-like bread. And it makes a good story, too!

    I like to make rolls with this recipe. The crust is soft and shiny, and the interior rich and
buttery. And when your guests are all commenting on the crumb, you get to tell them the fas-
cinating way these rolls are made.

Makes 12 rolls

½ cup warm water (100° to 115°F)

2¼ teaspoons (1 package) dry yeast

Pinch of sugar

½ cup whole milk, at room temperature

8 tablespoons (4 ounces) unsalted butter,
at room temperature

3 eggs

2 teaspoons kosher salt

3½ cups (1 pound, 1½ ounces) all-purpose flour

TOPPING:

1 egg

1 teaspoon poppyseeds

In a small bowl or glass, mix the water, yeast, and sugar together. Allow the mixture to bloom. It should become bubbly and smell yeasty, about 10 minutes.

In the bowl of a stand mixer fitted with the paddle attachment, add the milk, butter, eggs, salt, and 3 cups (15 ounces) of flour. At low speed, mix until just combined. Add the yeast mixture, and mix briefly.

Remove the paddle and attach the dough hook. With the mixer on low speed, begin kneading with the dough hook. Add the additional $\frac{1}{2}$ cup ($2\frac{1}{2}$ ounces) of flour. The dough will become a more cohesive mass, more elastic, and start to pull away from the sides of the bowl. This dough still will be quite tacky, but keep kneading until smooth, about 6 to 8 minutes.

Empty the dough out onto a well-floured surface, and scrape the bowl with a pastry scraper, adding any bits of dough to the mound. The dough will still be sticky; quickly work it into a loose ball. Place the dough onto a clean, well-floured tea towel or light kitchen towel (not terry cloth). Wrap the towel loosely (the cloth should allow room for the dough to grow), as you would a package, and tie it closed with kitchen twine. Fill your largest mixing bowl with warm water (100° to 115°F), and submerge the package of dough. The dough will sink at first. Let it set for about 45 minutes. The package will inflate and begin to float.

Lift the dough from the water, letting excess water drain off. Unwrap and scrape the dough out onto a lightly floured work surface. The dough will be quite wet and sticky. Knead to release the gases, folding the dough in each direction. (Using a plastic dough scraper is helpful in this case.) The dough will weigh about 2 pounds, 4 ounces. Divide it into 12 equally-sized pieces about 3 ounces each. Form each mound of dough into a roll shape (pages 83–84). Place on a parchment paper-lined baking tray.

Cover with another dry tea towel, and let the rolls rise for about 1 hour, or until almost doubled in bulk.

Arrange the oven rack in the middle of the oven. Fifteen minutes prior to baking, preheat to 375°F, and remove the tea towel from the tray. Before baking, make an egg wash by mixing the egg and 1 tablespoon water in a small bowl. Brush the surface of the rolls with egg wash, and then sprinkle with poppyseeds.

Bake for 20 to 23 minutes, or until golden brown. Enjoy while still warm, or cool to room temperature.

Bagels

IT SEEMS THAT NOWADAYS, YOU CAN PURCHASE A BAGEL IN JUST ABOUT EVERY CITY IN AMERICA. NOW these "bagels" may be hardly authentic. They may be bought on the bread aisle (or the freezer section) of the local supermarket, sealed in plastic. They may be flavored with chocolate chips, or tinted a dusty blue and flavored with blueberries. To me these sorts of bagels are just round breads with a hole. They are not the *true* boiled and then baked, chewy, oniony, Sunday morning carbohydrate of my people.

The bagel most likely originated in Poland, but along with Jewish rye bread, blintzes, and matzo ball soup, it was brought to this country and staunchly took root in Jewish-American culture. In the Lower East Side of Manhattan—a historically Jewish ghetto—there were over seventy bagel bakeries by 1900. Perhaps it was that this hand-held bread was practical. The pre-boiling gave the bread a longer shelf life, while contributing to the requisite chewy texture. The hole made the bagel easy to transport, slipping it on a rod or a rope—the way that it was thought to be originally carried.

It wasn't until the 1970s, when Murray Lender began to automate bagel production, selling a sweeter, lighter bagel to grocery stores, that the bagel began to lose its artisan appeal (see sidebar). So if you have been eating grocery store bagels, cast them aside. This recipe, toiled over and perfected by a true bagel connoisseur and dear friend of mine, Ian Quinn, is the closest thing to bagel nirvana as I have eaten since my time living in Manhattan. The dough is as it should be—stiff and heavy—and the directions are specific. But if followed, it'll be worth it! There is also a recipe for the ideal topping—Everything Mix—a mélange of poppy and sesame seeds, dried onion, and dried garlic, but any one topping is excellent as well. Just make these bagels; they're worth *kvelling* over.

Makes 12 bagels

1¾ cups warm water (100° to 115°F)

1 egg, beaten

3 tablespoons honey, plus 1 additional tablespoon added to the boiling water

2 teaspoons dry yeast

6 cups (1 pound, 14 ounces) all-purpose flour

1 tablespoon kosher salt

2 tablespoons coarse cornmeal

EVERYTHING MIX:

5 tablespoons minced dried onion

2 teaspoons minced dried garlic

2 tablespoons sesame seeds

2 tablespoons poppy seeds

In a large measuring cup, mix the water, egg, and 3 tablespoons of honey together until well-combined. Add the yeast, and stir briefly. Allow the mixture to bloom. It should become bubbly and smell yeasty, about 10 minutes.

In the bowl of a stand mixer fitted with the paddle attachment, add all of the flour and salt. Mix briefly just to combine. All at once, pour the yeast mixture into the flour mixture. With the mixer on low speed, stir just to combine.

Remove the paddle and attach the dough hook. With the mixer on low speed, begin kneading with the dough hook. The dough will be very stiff and heavy; continue to knead until the dough becomes very smooth and elastic, about 8 to 10 minutes. Empty it out onto a clean work surface. The dough will not require any additional flour. It should be rather dry and quite stiff. Knead the dough into a ball, and return it to the bowl. Wet a tea towel, and cover the dough completely. Allow it to rise for $1\frac{1}{2}$ to 2 hours, or until doubled in bulk.

Place the oven rack in the top third of the oven, and preheat to 450°F for 30 minutes prior to baking. Place a cast-iron skillet on the lower rack of the oven to preheat as well. The skillet will be used to create steam and a damp baking environment.

Prepare to form and boil the bagels:

Sprinkle the cornmeal evenly in a large, rimmed baking sheet. Set aside. Line another similarly sized pan with a cooling rack. Set aside.

In a small bowl, mix together the dried onion, dried garlic, sesame seeds, and poppy seeds for the topping. Set aside.

Fill a large 12- to 14-inch skillet with approximately 1 inch of water, and bring to a boil on the stove top.

Meanwhile, empty the dough out onto a clean work surface. Fold the dough over, once in each direction, to release the gases. Divide the dough in half. Each portion of dough should weigh approximately 1 pound, 5 ounces. Cover half of the dough with the moist towel while you are dividing the pieces. Form the dough into a circle. Divide the circle into 6 fairly equal-sized portions. Repeat with the other portion of dough. When you are finished, you will have 12 pieces of dough, weighing approximately 3½ ounces each. Cover the dough with the moist cloth while you are forming the bagels.

It is important that your work surface is clean and dry; you want to create friction, making the rolling process easier. Roll out one portion of dough into a cylinder about 12 inches in length. If at any time the dough becomes too difficult to roll out, leave it to rest, and the glutens will relax. Place one end of the dough rope under your palm, and wrap the dough loosely around your hand. The two ends should meet in your palm, overlapping by at least an inch. Place your palm down on the counter, apply a bit of pressure, and roll your hand over the ends, fusing together the circular shape that you have just created. Extract your hand. You will have a bagel shape; it is fine if the interior circle looks stretched or misshapen. Upon boiling and baking, a more uniform shape will be created. Repeat until 12 bagels are formed.

Add 1 tablespoon of honey to the boiling water. Add 3 or 4 bagels to the boiling water. Boil for approximately 30 seconds per side to gelatinize the exterior surface. The bagels will rise to the surface of the water when ready to be flipped. Remove them from the boiling water, and place them on the cooling rack-lined pan. Sprinkle both side of the bagels with the Everything Mix, then place the bagels snugly on the cornmeal-lined baking pan. One pan will hold all 12 bagels. Repeat until all of the bagels have been boiled and sprinkled with topping.

(At this point, you can retard the bagels—leave them to slowly rise in the refrigerator, and bake them the next day. The dough is however quite sticky, and should be covered well with freezer paper and then foil.)

Ready a cup with a few ice cubes. Place the bagels on the upper rack of the preheated oven. Quickly add the ice cubes to the skillet that has also been preheating on the lower rack, and shut the door immediately. Bake for 20 to 24 minutes, or until a deep, golden brown.

Remove the pan from the oven, and put the bagels in a large paper bag, folding over the opening. This steams the bagels, furthering the baking process. Cool in the bag until slightly warm or room temperature. The bagels are outstanding when freshly baked. By day two, they are best if frozen, and then thawed and toasted when desired.

Lender's Bagels

New Haven, Connecticut, my adopted hometown, is known for its pizza and a thriving Italian-American community. These Nutmeggers have become so comfortable with Italian ingredients, they have abbreviated the monikers into nicknames said with gusto. Mozzarella is *mozz*; prosciutto is *prozhoot;* and ricotta is *rigot*. Needless to say, for me, a Jewish girl hailing from the suburbs of San Francisco, I'm uncomfortable adopting this lingo as my own, and we don't have these nicknames for my cultural foods. What would I even call cream cheese and lox but cream cheese and lox? I thought that New Haven history was destined to leave me out. So imagine my surprise to discover, while researching the bagel, that Lender's Bagels, the ubiquitous grocery store bagel, originated in New Haven!

Lender's Bagels started as a small operation in New Haven when Harry Lender, an immigrant from Poland, bought a small bakery in the late 1920s. Originally, the bakery sold bread and just happened to sell bagels, too. But with the influx of other European immigrants in America, Lender saw a rise in his bagel sales. Bagels were filling a desire for that taste of home so many of his customers longed for. He upsized and opened New York Bagel Bakery. Still in New Haven, this was the first bagel bakery outside of Manhattan. He also began selling his bagels to other grocery stores throughout New England, marketing them as a Sunday morning specialty, as well as another form of sandwich rolls.

Business was booming, and three of Harry's four sons, Murray, Marvin, and Sam, joined with their father to make the bagel as ubiquitous in the rest of the country as it had become along the eastern seaboard. The answer to the problem of maintaining a fresh, chewy bagel many days after it has been baked? Why, freezing them, of course! We have the Lenders to thank for the large-scale mechanization of the bagel. They purchased the very first bagel-making machine—no more hand rolling necessary! They pre-sliced and then packaged the bagels—no knife was even needed before a bagel was slipped in the toaster! Eventually, the New York Bagel Bakery, a true small-scale operation, was closed and renamed Lender's Bagels, which carried the bagel into an age of automation.

Lender's Bagels was eventually sold to Kraft Foods, and it has since been sold a succession of times. It is bittersweet to know what has become of the bagel. Bitter in the sense that the frozen bagel, now bought at the grocery store, is hardly a bagel at all. These bagels have not been pre-boiled. They are too sweet. And where is the requisite chew? But sweet in the sense that what started as a humble food of immigrants has now gained such popularity and broad appeal in its new home.

SWEET ROLLS & BREADS

I HAVE NEVER MET A PERSON WHO DOES NOT HAVE A SOFT SPOT FOR SIN-
fully sweet breads. But no matter the quality of the bakery or restaurant, sweet rolls
are *never* as good as what you can make at home, and this chapter is testament to that.
Having a standout sweet roll recipe that you can turn to time and again is a necessity,
and you will find one in the Master Sweet Roll (page 108). This recipe will allow you
to make a variety of special treats, from warm Cinnamon Rolls (page 110) to decadent
Sticky Buns (page 113). For those times when a rich loaf is preferred, this chapter has
that covered too, with a Master Sweet Loaf (page 124) recipe. Decadent breads like
Peanut Butter and Jelly Swirl Bread (page 132) and the classic Cinnamon Raisin Swirl
Bread (page 126) are just waiting to be baked.

All of these breads will beckon sleepy denizens out of their beds with the aroma of
sweet yeast bread. I guarantee you will have a house full of happy diners.

Master Sweet Roll

EVERYONE NEEDS A SWEET ROLL RECIPE—A RECIPE THAT WILL MAKE CINNAMON ROLLS, STICKY BUNS, Monkey Bread, you name it! This one recipe is all that you need. It is dairy-rich and sweeter than most dough recipes in this book, but not cloyingly so. Better yet, it retards beautifully in the refrigerator, making fresh, hot sweet rolls possible first thing on a weekend morning.

¼ cup warm water (100° to 115°F)

2¼ teaspoons (1 package) dry yeast

Pinch of sugar

¾ cup whole milk, at room temperature

4 tablespoons (2 ounces) unsalted butter, at room temperature

¼ cup (1¾ ounces) sugar

2 eggs

2 teaspoons vanilla extract

1½ teaspoons kosher salt

3 to 3½ cups (15 ounces to 1 pound, 1½ ounces) all-purpose flour

In a small bowl or glass, mix the water, yeast, and sugar together. Allow the mixture to bloom. It should become bubbly and smell yeasty, about 10 minutes.

In the bowl of a stand mixer fitted with the paddle attachment, add the milk, butter, sugar, eggs, vanilla, salt, and 2 cups (10 ounces) of flour. At low speed, mix until just combined. Add the yeast mixture, and mix briefly. Continue to mix until it becomes web-like and more difficult to mix with the paddle attachment.

Remove the paddle and attach the dough hook. With the mixer on low speed, begin kneading with the dough hook, adding additional flour in ¼- to ½-cup increments. The dough will become a more cohesive mass, more elastic, and start to pull away from the sides of the bowl. It is important to watch the dough during this process. All of the flour should be incorporated at each step, but you don't want the dough to become too dry or heavy. Stop the mixer intermittently and touch the dough; it should still be tacky, but not too sticky. Sweet dough will be slightly stickier than other doughs, due to the sugar content. Dough will take anywhere from 1 to 1½ cups (5 to 7½ ounces) of additional flour. It should be smooth and free of lumps. This kneading process will take 6 to 10 minutes.

Empty the dough out onto a well-floured surface, scrape the bowl with a pastry scraper, adding any bits of dough from the bowl to the mound, and gently knead it into a ball. Put the dough back into the bowl, and place a piece of plastic wrap on the surface.

Place it in a warm spot, and let the dough rise 1½ to 2 hours, or until doubled in bulk.

Pull back the plastic wrap, and empty the dough out onto a well-floured surface. Fold the dough over, once in each direction, to release the gases. Form the dough into whichever shape is applicable for the recipe, and place the rolls in a prepared pan. Alternatively, place the pan, wrapped in plastic wrap, in the refrigerator to rise overnight. Then remove the pan from the refrigerator as you preheat the oven.

On Retarding Dough

Retarding, simply put, is refrigerating the dough during the rising and fermentation. The chilliness will not kill off the yeast, but rather make it sluggish and slow moving. Retarding can be done at two times in the baking process: during the bulk fermentation (the first rise) or after the shaping (the second rise). After the mixing and kneading, it is possible to set the dough in the refrigerator overnight for a slow initial rise. In the morning, let the dough warm slightly on the kitchen counter before continuing to shape and then bake the bread.

Yeast breads can be temperamental and time-consuming. While we all may want a gooey sticky bun on a Sunday morning, many of us don't want to wake up at 4 a.m. to begin baking them. So for many of the sweet roll recipes in this chapter, I recommend retarding the dough and baking off the rolls the next morning. It isn't necessary for the dough to be completely thawed; it will still bake beautifully with a slight chill.

It should also be noted that both of these processes can work in conjunction, or separately. Meaning, it's possible to start the bread-baking process Friday night, leave it to rise in the refrigerator during the bulk fermentation, shape the loaves or rolls Saturday, retard them overnight, and then have freshly baked bread Sunday morning. There are even some bakers who prefer this method. However you chose to bake your bread, just remember—you are in charge! Make the baking enjoyable for *you*, and the final product will be all the sweeter.

Cinnamon Rolls

CINNAMON ROLLS ARE AN EXERCISE IN BALANCE—THEY SHOULD BE WARM YET NOT HOT, THE BREAD needs to be sturdy yet buoyant, the filling gooey but not messy.

They are not the type of roll that one has every morning. They're probably not even the type of roll one has every month. (If you *are* eating a home baked cinnamon roll every month—tell me where you live, I'm coming over!) In short, when I have a cinnamon roll, I want it to be perfect. It's a sweet roll, so yes, I want it to be somewhat sweet, but I also want it to be spicy and warm. I want my cinnamon rolls slathered in a rich, white glaze. I want to think that I could eat the entire pan, but after just one, I want to be fully satisfied. That's a lot of requirements for one roll to live up to, but I believe this one does.

You'll see that the filling is a basic brown sugar-cinnamon one. I don't want to mess with perfection, and the spice is just right. For the glaze, I've gone with cream cheese. Room temperature cream cheese is the perfect vehicle for making a rich, fluffy topping with just a hint of tang. I have also scented this glaze with a bit of orange zest. You'll notice that I've used the used the word "scented" rather than "flavored." The orange zest simply hints at brightness; it won't hit you over the head with a citrus impact. In fact, there is no single starring ingredient in this recipe; it's the coalescence that makes one superb morning treat!

Makes 12 rolls

I recipe Master Sweet Roll (page 108)
I tablespoon unsalted butter, melted

½ cup (3 ounces) brown sugar

3 teaspoons cinnamon

Pinch of kosher salt

GLAZE:

¼ pound (4 ounces) cream cheese,
at room temperature

2 tablespoons (1 ounce) unsalted butter, at room temperature

Pinch of kosher salt

¾ cup (3¼ ounces) confectioners' sugar

1 teaspoon vanilla extract

½ teaspoon grated orange zest

Follow the Master Sweet Roll recipe through the first rise.

Grease a 13 x 9-inch pan with the melted butter, and set aside.

In a small bowl, make the filling by thoroughly combining the brown sugar, cinnamon, and salt. Set aside.

On a well-floured work surface, empty the dough out. Fold the dough over, once in each direction, to release the gases. With a rolling pin, roll the dough out to approximately 16 x 10 inches. Brush the surface of the dough with room temperature water. Sprinkle the filling over the dough, leaving ½ inch of space on the longer sides of the dough. Press the filling lightly into the dough. Roll it tightly to form a cylinder 16 inches long. Pinch the final seam of dough to the cylinder, closing the roll. Gently roll the cylinder back and forth to make sure that it is amply secure and moves easily from the counter.

With a sharp knife or pastry cutter, cut the dough into 12 equal pieces, a little over 1-inch in length. Place each roll in the pan, leaving a bit of room between rolls. They will continue to rise.

Cover the pan with plastic wrap, and let the rolls rise at room temperature until doubled in bulk, 1 to 1½ hours. You may also cover them in plastic wrap and leave them to rise overnight in the refrigerator.

Arrange the oven rack in the middle of the oven. Fifteen minutes prior to baking, preheat to 400°F. If the rolls have been refrigerated, remove them from the refrigerator a half hour before baking, while the oven is preheating.

Remove plastic wrap, and bake the rolls for 20 to 25 minutes. They should be golden brown.

Remove the pan from the oven, and set it on a cooling rack to cool for about a half hour. While the rolls are cooling, make the glaze.

In the bowl of a stand mixer fitted with a whisk attachment, beat the cream cheese and the butter until smooth. Add the salt and the confectioners' sugar, and continue to beat until shiny and smooth. Lastly, add the vanilla extract and the orange zest, and mix to combine.

With an off-set spatula, spread the glaze onto the cinnamon rolls. The rolls will still be warm, so some of the glaze will melt right onto the cinnamon rolls. Enjoy right away!

Brushing Dough with Water

Throughout this chapter you will notice one glaring omission— an excess of butter. Don't get me wrong; I love the fat and use it in abundance. I just do not call for butter to be slathered on the interior of doughs and then rolled into swirls. I took a bread-making class awhile back in which the instructor advised against using butter for this task. Her reasoning was this: One uses butter to grease pans—it creates nonstick surfaces. So used as a filling, it contributes to slippery doughs and messy swirls. It makes sense, doesn't it? By brushing the surface of the dough with water, you make the dough tacky again—the perfect medium for adhering spices, sugar, chocolate, or whatever you intend on swirling in your bread. This method is neater. It will not have you trying to stick errant blobs of goo back into your dough. And I promise, you won't even miss that extra bit of butter. You'll be too busy consuming melted chocolate or sweet caramel to even notice!

Sticky Buns

MY MOTHER USED TO HAVE *THE* STICKY BUN RECIPE. SWEET, BUT NOT TOOTH-ACHINGLY SO, WITH toasty pecans and just the right amount of stickiness to make eating them seem slightly naughty. The recipe was originally from the back of a yeast packet. My mother had transcribed it onto a piece of paper, and it was slipped inside a binder with all of her most-cherished recipes. Just which brand of yeast it came from has been long forgotten, but the recipe was well loved. These buns were a special treat, and a few times a year my mom would mix up a batch. This was an all-day affair, culminating in a sticky bun dessert on Sunday evening.

My mother is not the type of devious cook who omits secret ingredients from recipes before she gives them to friends. She is free with her recipes and advice—perhaps too free. She lent her copy of the sticky bun recipe to a neighbor that had fallen hard for my mother's sweet rolls, and the neighbor in turn lost the recipe. *The* sticky bun recipe was gone forever. Through the years, my mom had tried different recipes, but they were not the same—the buns were good, but they were not *great*.

When I began writing this book, I knew that it would have to include this American classic. I also knew that the recipe would have to be stellar; I would be replacing the ultimate recipe from my past. So, after much toiling, this is *the* recipe. With only the suggestion of cinnamon, these rolls are indeed all about the pecans. Prior to baking I roast the nuts, giving them that added toasty flavor. The topping is just sticky enough, flowing over the buns. These sticky buns are great on their own, but for a modern, salty-sweet combination, try them with a sprinkling of coarse salt on top—it brings these sticky buns to the next level!

Makes 16 buns

1 recipe Master Sweet Roll (page 108)

¾ cup (3 ounces) pecans

1 tablespoon (½ ounce) unsalted butter, melted

GLAZE:

8 tablespoons (4 ounces) unsalted butter

1 cup (6 ounces) brown sugar

¼ cup dark corn syrup

¼ teaspoon kosher salt

FILLING:

2 tablespoons sugar

2 tablespoons brown sugar, packed

1 teaspoon ground cinnamon

Pinch of kosher salt

Sprinkling of coarse salt,
such as Maldon (optional)

Follow the Master Sweet Roll recipe through the first rise.

Preheat oven to 350°F.

Place the pecans on a small baking pan and roast for 8 to 10 minutes, or until toasty and fragrant. Remove the pecans from the oven, let them cool slightly, and then coarsely chop them. Set them aside.

Grease two 8- or 9-inch round cake pans with the melted butter, and set aside.

To make the glaze, put the butter, brown sugar, corn syrup, and salt in a small saucepan. Over medium heat, cook until the butter is melted and the mixture begins to boil and bubble, about 2 minutes. Swirling the contents of the pan, simmer the glaze for about 1 minute, making sure the sugar and corn syrup are liquefied and blended. Pour half the glaze into each of the cake pans, swirling them to make sure they are evenly coated. Sprinkle the coarsely chopped pecans evenly over the glaze. Set aside.

In a small bowl, make the filling by thoroughly combining the sugars, cinnamon, and salt. Set aside.

On a well-floured work surface, empty the dough out. Fold the dough over, once in each direction, to release the gases. Roll the dough out to approximately 18 x 12 inches. Brush the surface of the dough with room temperature water. Sprinkle the filling evenly over the surface of the dough, leaving $\frac{1}{2}$-inch of space on the longer sides of the dough. Press the filling lightly into the dough. Roll it tightly to form a cylinder 18 inches long. Pinch the final seam of dough to the cylinder, closing the roll. Gently roll the cylinder back and forth to make sure that it is amply secure and moves easily from the counter.

With a sharp knife or pastry cutter, cut the dough in half. Cut each half into 8 equal pieces. Place each roll into the cake pans, 8 per pan, leaving a bit of room between the rolls. They will continue to rise.

Cover the pans with plastic wrap or a tea towel, and let the rolls rise at room temperature until doubled in bulk, 1 to $1\frac{1}{2}$ hours. You may also cover them in plastic wrap, and leave them to rise overnight in the refrigerator.

Arrange the oven rack in the middle of the oven, and fifteen minutes prior to baking, preheat to 350°F. If rolls have been refrigerated, remove them from the refrigerator a half hour before baking, while the oven is preheating.

Remove the plastic wrap or tea towel, and bake for 30 to 35 minutes. The rolls should be golden brown and the glaze bubbling.

Remove the buns from the oven, and on a cooling rack, immediately turn the cake pans over. Leave the pans upside-down over the rolls, letting the glaze and the nuts drip over them. After about 5 minutes, remove the pans. If using, sprinkle the buns with coarse salt, then let the rolls cool slightly. Enjoy them while they're still warm.

Dakota Rolls

IMAGINE THE AUSTERE CHARACTER OF A NORTH DAKOTA WINTER. NEXT, IMAGINE A GLOSSY SWEET roll. Now combine these two images together. That's a Dakota Roll! I like to think of these rolls as a sticky bun *light*—nothing is overpowering about them, and they show a certain amount of restraint. Made like a traditional sticky bun, with melty brown sugar on the inside and lacquered in a gooey mixture of more brown sugar and a few tablespoons of butter, a Dakota Roll may appear far from austere. But one bite into these soft rolls, still warm from the oven, and you'll know what I mean in using the word "light" to describe them. They are not too sweet, not too buttery, not over the top. These rolls may be a little like a good, old North Dakota farmer—sturdy, honest, and to the point!

I've modified the recipe by substituting honey for the traditional ingredient, corn syrup. The honey lends an old-fashioned taste to the sweet rolls. It will harden as the rolls cool, creating a pleasant, crackly topping, but I recommend eating these rolls still warm and straight from the oven.

Makes 16 rolls

I recipe Master Sweet Roll (page 108)
I tablespoon (½ ounce) unsalted butter, melted

GLAZE:

4 tablespoons (2 ounces) unsalted butter
¾ cup (4½ ounces) brown sugar, packed
3 tablespoons honey
Pinch of kosher salt

FILLING:

¼ cup (1½ ounces) brown sugar, packed

Follow the Master Sweet Roll recipe through the first rise.

Grease two 8- or 9-inch round cake pans with the melted butter, and set aside.

To make the glaze, put the butter, brown sugar, honey, and salt in a small saucepan. Over medium heat, cook until the butter is melted and the mixture begins to boil, about

2 minutes. Swirling the contents of the pan, simmer the glaze for about 1 minute, making sure the sugar and honey are liquefied and blended. Pour the glaze equally into each of the cake pans, swirling the pans to make sure they are evenly coated with the glaze. Set aside.

On a well-floured work surface, empty the dough out. Fold the dough over, once in each direction, to release the gases. Roll it out to approximately 18 x 12 inches. Brush the surface of the dough with room temperature water. Sprinkle the brown sugar filling evenly over the surface of the dough, leaving $1/2$ inch of space on the longer sides of the dough. Press the filling lightly into the dough. Roll it tightly to form a cylinder 18 inches long. Pinch the final seam of dough to the cylinder, closing the roll. Gently roll the cylinder back and forth to make sure that it is amply secure and moves easily from the counter.

With a sharp knife or pastry cutter, cut the dough in half. Cut each half into 8 equal pieces. Place each roll into the cake pans, 8 per pan, leaving a bit of room between the rolls. They will continue to rise.

Cover the pans with plastic wrap or a tea towel, and let the rolls rise at room temperature until doubled in bulk, 1 to $1^{1}/2$ hours. You may also cover them in plastic wrap and leave them to rise overnight in the refrigerator.

Arrange the oven rack in the middle of the oven, and fifteen minutes prior to baking, preheat to 375°F. If the rolls have been refrigerated, remove them from the refrigerator a half hour before baking, while the oven is preheating.

Remove the plastic wrap or tea towel, and bake for 25 to 30 minutes. The rolls should be golden brown and the glaze bubbling.

Remove the rolls from the oven, and on a cooling rack, immediately turn the cake pans over. Leave the pans upside down over the rolls, letting the glaze drip over them. After about 5 minutes, remove the pans, and let the rolls cool slightly. Enjoy while still warm.

Sweet Dutch Crunch

THIS RECIPE IS A BIT OF A MASH-UP. NESTLED UNDER A CINNAMON-SCENTED, CRISPY DUTCH CRUNCH topping is an eggy and rich, chocolate-flecked bun—the perfect sweet roll with which to say "good morning."

The Dutch Crunch topping does not have to be relegated to simply rolls, or even a loaf of bread. This shatteringly crisp crust is the ideal vehicle to coat a sweet bun as well. The Master Sweet Roll recipe gets a tiny makeover by the addition of bittersweet chocolate chips, and the Dutch Crunch topping comes alive with the a taste of cinnamon. The bittersweet chocolate is just sumptuous enough, while the topping and the roll are complementary—making this roll a standout.

Makes 12 rolls

I recipe Master Sweet Roll (page 108)
I tablespoon (½ ounce) unsalted butter, melted
I cup (5 ounces) bittersweet chocolate chips

TOPPING:
I recipe Dutch Crunch topping (page 90)
¼ teaspoon cinnamon

Follow the Master Sweet Roll recipe, allowing it to rise partially for about 1 hour. Then make the paste for the topping.

In a medium-size bowl, whisk the yeast, sugar, salt, rice flour, and cinnamon together, until combined. Add the oil and the water, and continue to whisk until well-incorporated. The mixture should be smooth and free of lumps. It should have a paste-like consistency. Allow it to rise until the sweet bread is finished proofing, about one half hour.

Grease a 13 x 9-inch pan with the melted butter, and set aside.

On a well-floured work surface, empty out the dough. Fold the dough over, once in each direction, to release the gases. Knead the chocolate chips evenly into the dough. Divide into 12 equally-sized pieces, weighing approximately 3 ounces each. Form each mound of dough into a roll shape (pages 83–84). Place in the prepared baking pan.

The topping will have risen substantially. With a spoon, stir the mixture down. Spoon the topping onto the rolls, letting it drip down the sides. The topping should not only cover the tops of the rolls, but the sides as well. There will be just enough topping to completely cover the rolls.

Let the rolls rise for about 1 hour, or until almost doubled in bulk.

Arrange the oven rack in the middle of the oven, and fifteen minutes prior to baking, preheat to 375°F.

Bake for 30 to 35 minutes, or until the rolls are crackly and golden brown. Remove the rolls from the oven, and set them on a cooling rack for approximately 5 minutes. Let the rolls cool slightly; they are best eaten while still warm.

STICKY FINGERS

There are times when baking bread that your hands get covered in dough—it's just a hazard of the job. How do you get this sticky mess off? I've found that washing your hands can be futile. The dough gets wet, slippery, and sludgy, and you look at your hands afterward and still find dough clinging steadfastly to your fingers.

The best way to clean off your hands after encountering a persistent ball of dough is not with soap and water, but rather with flour. The same principle is at work in flouring your work surface as it is in flouring your hands—dough sticks to dough; it does not stick to flour. Take a spoonful of flour in your hands, and rub them briskly over the trashcan. You will see that, as you continue to rub, your hands will get cleaner, and the dough will fall into the can. While your hands may not be spick and span, they will certainly be nonstick. Many professional bakers do not let water touch their hands until they are through with all of the day's baking. They just continue to clean their hands with flour. While I can't recommend that, the next time you find yourself in a sticky situation, give flouring a try.

Monkey Bread

MONKEY BREAD IS ONE OF THOSE DECADENT BREAKFAST TREATS THAT BEGAN APPEARING IN AMERICAN women's magazines in the 1950s. A cross between a non-fried, sugar-dusted donut hole and a gooey cinnamon roll, eating this bread is a communal activity. Baked in a tube or Bundt pan, this bread is a jumble of bread bites, discretely rolled in butter, then cinnamon-sugar, and piled one on top of the other. The spicy smell wafting from the oven will taunt you. And once it's finished baking, you will be hurrying to unmold it and behold your sticky, beautiful mess—before pulling off a chunk to enjoy. I have adorned this morning treat with a buttermilk glaze. Drizzled on top, this glaze keeps the bread moist, while the buttermilk adds just a hint of tanginess.

Monkey Bread is really best the day that is baked, but if you some left over, there is a recipe for a decadent Monkey Bread Pudding (page 206) that is another way to enjoy this sweet treat.

Makes 1 large Bundt pan or tube pan

1 recipe Master Sweet Roll (page 108)
1 tablespoon (½ ounce) unsalted butter, melted

CINNAMON-SUGAR COATING:

4 tablespoons (2 ounces) unsalted butter, melted
½ cup (3 ounces) brown sugar
¼ cup (1¾ ounces) sugar
2 teaspoons ground cinnamon
¼ teaspoon kosher salt

BUTTERMILK GLAZE:

½ cup (2¼ ounces) confectioners' sugar
1 tablespoon buttermilk
½ teaspoon vanilla
Pinch of kosher salt

Follow the Master Sweet Roll recipe through the first rise.

Grease a large Bundt pan or tube pan with the melted butter, and set aside.

To make the coating, place the melted butter in a small bowl. In another bowl, thoroughly mix both the sugars, cinnamon, and salt together. Set both bowls aside.

On a well-floured work surface, empty out the dough. Fold the dough over, once in each direction, to release the gases. Using a knife or dough scraper, slice the dough into approximately 64 pieces. It is fine if these pieces are not exactly the same size; you want the disparity. Roll each piece into a ball of dough. Using a fork or by hand, dunk each ball into the butter, and then roll it in the cinnamon-sugar mixture. Place the dough balls into the pan, staggering them to create a cake-like mass of dough balls when complete.

Cover the pan with plastic wrap, and let the dough balls rise at room temperature until doubled in bulk, and about 1 to 2 inches from the top of the pan, approximately 1 hour. Alternately, you may also cover the bread in plastic wrap, and leave it to rise overnight in the refrigerator.

Fifteen minutes prior to baking, preheat the oven to 350°F. If the rolls have been refrigerated, remove them from the refrigerator a half hour before baking, while the oven is preheating.

Remove the plastic wrap, and bake for 30-35 minutes, until golden brown. Remove the pan from the oven, and allow it to cool for 5 minutes. Turn it out onto a platter; cool for 5 additional minutes.

Meanwhile, make the buttermilk glaze. In a bowl, whisk the confectioners' sugar, buttermilk, vanilla, and salt together until smooth. With a spoon, drizzle the glaze over the warm Monkey Bread. Some of the glaze will soak into the bread. Any additional glaze may be served alongside.

NOTE: If using a tube pan, it is important that the pan be solid, not one with a removable base. The cinnamon-sugar mixture will become molten and caramelize, seeping out of the bottom of a pan that is not secure.

Sugar Crusted Rolls

THE FARM JOURNAL'S *HOMEMADE BREAD*, PUBLISHED IN 1969, IS A TREASURE. THIS OUT-OF-PRINT volume is a collection of recipes from around the country that were developed, tested, and shared by farm women. They are generally hearty, not too complicated, and well, a little out-of-date—but I still love glancing through the pages. Reading the recipes is truly taking a look back into our food culture. When I saw the recipe for Sugar Crusted Rolls—essentially a sweet crescent roll, I knew I would have to give it a try. When I baked it, the recipe fell a bit flat. The dough was dull, and while sugar crusting seems like a good idea, the caramelizing of the final product verged on burnt sugar. It left an acrid taste in my mouth, not a pleasingly sweet one. The recipe was screaming out for modernization, begging to be reintroduced!

What I share with you now is Sugar Crusted Rolls *inspired* by Farm Journal. I brightened the dough with freshly grated lemon zest. I have also further sweetened my Master Sweet Roll recipe, because in my recipe, the sugar crusting is just on the top of the rolls. The "crusting" has been replaced by a healthy sprinkling of sanding sugar—a finishing sugar. Coarser and more sparkling than even turbinado, it won't melt upon baking and has a pleasing crunch. However, if you can't find sanding sugar, go ahead and use turbinado, or Sugar in the Raw.

Makes 16 crescent rolls

I recipe Master Sweet Roll (page 108)

¼ cup (1¾ ounces) sugar

¼ to ½ cup (1¼ to 2½ ounces) all-purpose flour

2 tablespoons grated lemon zest
(from approximately 2 lemons)

I egg

I tablespoon sanding sugar

Follow the Master Sweet Roll recipe, adding ¼ cup of additional sugar, through mixing with the paddle attachment.

Switch to the dough hook, and begin the kneading process. This may require ¼ to ½ cup (1¼ to 2½ ounces) additional flour. As the dough begins to come together, but still is a bit sticky, add the lemon zest. Continue to knead, adding more flour if necessary, until the dough is smooth and free of lumps. This kneading process will take 6 to 10 minutes.

Empty the dough out onto a well-floured surface, scrape the bowl with a pastry scraper, adding any bits of dough from the bowl to the mound, and gently knead it into a ball. Put it back into the bowl, and place a piece of plastic wrap on the surface of the dough.

Place it in a warm spot, and let the dough rise 1½ to 2 hours, or until doubled in bulk.

Pull back the plastic wrap, and empty out the dough onto a well-floured surface. Fold the dough over, once in each direction, to release the gases. Divide the dough in half; each half will be a little over 1 pound.

On a well-floured surface, roll the dough out into a 12-inch circle, approximately ⅓ inch thick. Slice the circle into 8 equal wedges. Starting with the broad base, roll the dough into a crescent shape; to secure, tuck the point under the roll. Form crescents with the rest of the dough, then arrange them on a parchment-lined baking sheet. Repeat the process with the other portion of dough, arranging the crescents on a separate baking pan.

Cover the pans with a tea towel, and allow the crescent rolls to rise approximately 1½ hours. You may also cover them in plastic wrap and leave them to rise overnight in the refrigerator.

Arrange the oven racks to the center of the oven, and fifteen minutes prior to baking, preheat to 375°F. If the rolls have been refrigerated, remove them from the refrigerator a half hour before baking, while the oven is preheating.

Before baking, make an egg wash by mixing the egg and 1 tablespoon water in a small bowl. Remove the plastic wrap or tea towel, brush the surface of the rolls with egg wash, and then sprinkle with the sanding sugar.

Bake for 18 to 22 minutes, rotating the pans once at the halfway point.

Remove the pans from the oven, and set them on a cooling rack for approximately 5 minutes. Remove the rolls from the pans, and cool slightly. Enjoy the crescents while they're still warm.

Master Sweet Loaf

WHEN I WANT TO BAKE ONE OF THOSE IMPRESSIVE LOAVES OF BREAD WITH AN INTRICATE, GOOEY swirl within, this is the recipe I turn to. Slightly leaner than the Master Sweet Roll recipe, this dough is a moderately sweet, white loaf. It takes a back seat to whichever ingredients you want swirling around beneath the crust. Rich with buttermilk, this bread is delicious on its own, but it can make decadent French toast as well. Following the recipe for the Master Loaf are a handful of recipes to make a stellar swirl, but I invite you to do some delicious experimentation, too.

Makes 1 loaf

¼ cup warm water (100° to 115°F)

2¼ teaspoons (1 package) dry yeast

Pinch of sugar

¾ cup buttermilk, at room temperature

2 tablespoons (1 ounce) unsalted butter,
at room temperature

3 tablespoons sugar

1 teaspoon vanilla extract

1 teaspoon kosher salt

2 to 2½ cups (10 to 12½ ounces) all-purpose flour

In a small bowl or glass, mix the water, yeast, and sugar together. Allow the mixture to bloom. It should become bubbly and smell yeasty, about 10 minutes.

In the bowl of a stand mixer fitted with the paddle attachment, add the buttermilk, butter, sugar, vanilla, salt, and 1 cup (5 ounces) of flour. At low speed, mix until just combined. Add the yeast mixture, and mix briefly. Add another ½ cup (2½ ounces) of flour, and continue to mix at low speed until the mixture becomes web-like and more difficult to mix with the paddle attachment.

Remove the paddle and attach the dough hook. With the mixer on low speed, begin kneading with the dough hook, adding additional flour in ¼-cup increments. The dough will become a more cohesive mass, more elastic, and start to pull away from the sides of the bowl. It is important to watch the dough during this process. All of the flour should be incorporated at each step, but you don't want the dough to become too dry or heavy. Stop the mixer intermittently and touch the dough; it should still be tacky, but not too sticky. The dough will take anywhere from $\frac{1}{2}$ to 1 cup ($2\frac{1}{2}$ to 5 ounces) of additional flour. It should be smooth and free of lumps. This kneading process will take 6 to 10 minutes.

Empty the dough out onto a well-floured surface, scrape the bowl with a pastry scraper, adding any bits of dough from the bowl to the mound, and gently knead it into a ball. Put it back into the bowl, and place a piece of plastic wrap on the surface of the dough.

Place it in a warm spot, and let the dough rise $1\frac{1}{2}$ to 2 hours, or until doubled in bulk.

Pull back the plastic wrap, and empty the dough out onto a well-floured surface. Fold the dough over, once in each direction, to release the gases. Roll the dough out to approximately 11 x 8 inches. Spread the filling evenly over the dough, leaving $\frac{1}{2}$ inch of space on the longer sides of the dough. Roll the dough tightly to form a cylinder 11 inches long. Pinch the final seam of dough to the cylinder, closing the roll. Tuck the ends under, and place it in a loaf pan.

Cover the pan with plastic wrap or a tea towel, and let the loaf rise for 1 to $1\frac{1}{2}$ hours, or until doubled in bulk. It is fine if the bread is not quite cresting the lip of the pan before baking. Because of the swirled interior, you will want a more contained loaf of bread.

Arrange the oven rack in the middle of the oven, and fifteen minutes prior to baking, preheat to 350°F.

Remove the plastic wrap or tea towel, place the pan in the center of the oven, and bake for approximately 35 to 40 minutes, rotating once at the halfway point.

Remove the pan from the oven, and set it on a cooling rack for approximately 5 minutes. Release the loaf from its pan, and allow it to cool to room temperature before enjoying.

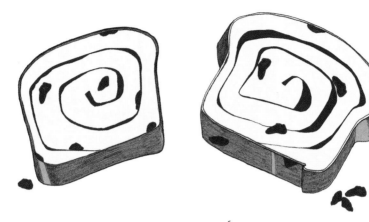

Cinnamon Raisin Swirl Bread

THIS CLASSIC BREAD MAKES WONDERFUL TOAST, SUPERB FRENCH TOAST, AND FOR THAT SALTY-SWEET combination, an enticing grilled cheese. This loaf is chock full of raisins that have been soaked in boiling water to both rehydrate them and to prevent them from scorching during the baking process. In my recipe, the raisins are kneaded throughout the entire loaf, not simply swirled in the center of the bread. If I'm going to make a raisin bread, I want my raisins throughout!

Makes 1 loaf

½ cup (2½ ounces) raisins
1 cup boiling water
1 recipe Master Sweet Loaf (page 124)

FILLING:
¼ cup (1½ ounces) brown sugar, packed
2½ teaspoons cinnamon

EGG WASH:
1 egg

Soak the raisins in 1 cup boiling water for 15 to 30 minutes. Drain well. As you are making the dough, add the raisins when the dough has almost come together, and the last $\frac{1}{2}$ cup ($2\frac{1}{2}$ ounces) of flour is being added. Proceed with the recipe for the Master Sweet Loaf through the first rise.

In a small bowl, make the filling by mixing together the brown sugar and the cinnamon. Set aside. Pull back the plastic wrap, and empty the dough out onto a well-floured surface. Fold the dough over, once in each direction, to release the gases. Roll the dough out to approximately 11 x 8 inches. Brush the surface of the dough with room temperature water. Spread the filling evenly over the dough, leaving $\frac{1}{2}$ inch of space on the longer sides of the dough. Roll the dough tightly to form a cylinder 11 inches long. Pinch the final seam of dough to the cylinder, closing the roll. Tuck the ends under, and place in a loaf pan.

Cover the pan with plastic wrap, and let the loaf rise for 1 to $1\frac{1}{2}$ hours, or until doubled in bulk. It is fine if the bread is not quite cresting the lip of the pan before baking. Because of the swirled interior, you will want a more contained loaf of bread.

Arrange the oven rack in the middle of the oven, and fifteen minutes prior to baking, preheat to 350°F.

In a small bowl, mix the egg and 1 tablespoon water together. Remove the plastic wrap, and brush the egg wash on the top of the loaf.

Place the pan in the center of the oven and bake for approximately 35 to 40 minutes, rotating once at the halfway point.

Remove the pan from the oven, and set it on a cooling rack for approximately 5 minutes. Release the loaf from its pan, and allow it to cool to room temperature before enjoying.

Chocolate Swirl Bread with Crumb Topping

THIS IS NOT THE TYPE OF BREAD TO SLICE FOR SANDWICHES; I'M NOT EVEN SO SURE THAT IT NEEDS a slathering of butter. This is the type of bread to relish on a Sunday morning—and maybe even into the afternoon as well. A basic swirl bread, it is intertwined with chopped bits of chocolate. When eaten warm, the chocolate is melty and wonderfully messy, and when eaten at room temperature, the chocolate has the opportunity to harden, becoming chewy and flavorful. The crowning achievement of the bread is the crumb topping. Similar to that sweet crumb topping on New York-style crumb cakes, upon baking it provides a crisp, sweet shell to the soft, chocolaty interior of the bread. Before baking, brush the bread with water and pat on the crumb topping. I suggest setting an empty baking pan on the lower rack of the oven. This pan can catch any crumbs that may tumble from the loaf during baking and save you from having to clean a messy oven. Don't worry though, plenty of delicious crumbs will remain on the bread!

Makes 1 loaf

1 recipe Master Sweet Loaf (page 124)

FILLING:

2½ ounces semisweet or bittersweet chocolate, chopped

2 tablespoons brown sugar, packed

½ teaspoon cinnamon

Pinch of kosher salt

CRUMB TOPPING:

⅓ cup (1⅔ ounces) all-purpose flour

2 tablespoons sugar

2 tablespoons brown sugar, packed

¼ teaspoon kosher salt

3 tablespoons (1½ ounces) unsalted butter, melted

Proceed with the recipe for the Master Sweet Loaf through the first rise.

In a small bowl, make the filling by mixing together the chocolate, brown sugar, cinnamon, and salt. Set aside. Pull back the plastic wrap, and empty the dough out onto a well-floured surface. Fold the dough over, once in each direction, to release the gases. Roll the dough out to approximately 11 x 8 inches. Brush the surface of the dough with room temperature water. Spread the filling evenly over the dough, leaving $\frac{1}{2}$ inch of space on the longer sides of the dough. Roll the dough tightly to form a cylinder 11 inches long. Pinch the final seam of dough to the cylinder, closing the roll. Tuck the ends under, and place it in a loaf pan.

Cover the pan with plastic wrap or a tea towel, and let the loaf rise for 1 to $1\frac{1}{2}$ hours, or until doubled in bulk. Meanwhile, make the crumb topping. In a medium-size bowl, whisk the flour, sugar, brown sugar, and salt together. Pour in the melted butter. Quickly stir the butter into flour mixture, moistening it completely. The topping may begin to clump; simply break the clumps apart into a manageable crumb-size topping. Set aside. You want the crumb mixture to have time to rest and dry out some.

Arrange the oven rack in the middle of the oven, and fifteen minutes prior to baking, preheat to 350°F.

Remove the plastic wrap from the pan. Brush the surface of the loaf with room temperature water, and pat on the crumb topping. The crumbs will almost completely cover the loaf.

Place an empty baking pan on the lower rack of the oven to catch any falling crumbs. Place the loaf pan in the center of the oven and bake for approximately 50 to 55 minutes, rotating once at the halfway point.

Remove the loaf from the oven, and set on a cooling rack for approximately 5 minutes. Release the loaf from its pan, and allow it to cool. Loaf may be enjoyed while still warm.

Orange Swirl Loaf with Cherries and Pecans

ORANGES CAN BRIGHTEN UP EVEN THE DREARIEST OF WINTERS, AS THE FAMOUS ORANGE-PRODUCING states, California and Florida, know too well. With one measly orange, this bread packs a lot of citrusy punch. Using the Master Sweet Loaf augmented with orange zest, this bread also has an interior swirl of jammy dried cherries and toasty pecans. Squeeze the fruit for an orange juice glaze, and you've got one impressive-looking, delicious-tasting loaf of bread that chases away the cold weather with every bite.

Makes 1 loaf

2 teaspoons orange zest

3 tablespoons orange juice, freshly squeezed

I recipe Master Sweet Loaf (page 124)

FILLING:

¼ cup (I ounce) pecans

⅓ cup (1¾ ounces) dried cherries

I cup boiling water

¼ cup (1¾ ounces) sugar

2 tablespoons brown sugar, packed

Pinch of salt

GLAZE:

I cup (4½ ounces) confectioners' sugar, sifted

I tablespoon (½ ounce) unsalted butter, melted

2 to 3 tablespoons orange juice

Add the orange zest and juice as you are adding the ingredients to the stand mixer, and then proceed with the recipe for the Master Sweet Loaf through the first rise.

Preheat the oven to 350°F. Place the pecans on a small baking pan, and roast for 8 to 10 minutes, or until toasty and fragrant. Remove the pecans from the oven, let them cool slightly, and then chop them. Set aside. Pour 1 cup boiling water over the cherries and soak for 15 to 30 minutes. Drain well, and finely chop.

In a small bowl, make the filling by mixing together the nuts, cherries, sugar, brown sugar, and salt. Set aside. Pull back the plastic wrap, and empty the dough out onto a well-floured surface. Fold the dough over, once in each direction, to release the gases. Roll the dough out to approximately 11 x 8 inches. Brush the surface of the dough with room temperature water. Spread the filling evenly over the dough, leaving $1/2$ inch of space on the longer sides of the dough. Roll the dough tightly to form a cylinder 11 inches long. Pinch the final seam of dough to the cylinder, closing the roll. Tuck the ends under, and place it in a loaf pan.

Cover the pan with plastic wrap or a tea towel, and let the loaf rise for 1 to $1\frac{1}{2}$ hours, or until doubled in bulk. (It is fine if the bread is not quite cresting the lip of the pan before baking. Because of the swirled interior, you will want a more contained loaf.)

Arrange the oven rack in the middle of the oven, and fifteen minutes prior to baking, preheat to 350°F.

Remove the plastic wrap, and place the pan in the center of the oven and bake for approximately 35 to 40 minutes, rotating once at the halfway point.

Remove the pan from the oven, and set it on a cooling rack for approximately 5 minutes. Release the loaf from its pan, and allow it to cool to room temperature.

Make the glaze. In a small bowl, mix together the confectioners' sugar, butter, and juice. The glaze should be fluid and lump-free. Set a piece of wax paper underneath the cooling rack to catch any overflow Pour the glaze over the top of the bread. Allow it to harden for 1 hour, and then enjoy.

Peanut Butter and Jelly Swirl Bread

WHAT MORE CAN BE SAID ABOUT THIS PERENNIAL FAVORITE, EXCLUSIVELY AMERICAN COMBINATION that hasn't been said before? People have a soft spot for PB&J. Adults may sneak a sandwich from time to time, but I say, be proud of this love affair! Eat with abandon! I even made a recipe for a bread with those two delicious flavors swirled right in! By smearing salty peanut butter and sweet jelly in alternating stripes within the dough, rolling it tightly, then baking it in a loaf pan, you get peanut butter and jelly bread. Once cooled, I put a confectioners' sugar glaze on top, and then sprinkle the loaf with finely chopped, salted peanuts. This bread really doesn't require another thing. Simply enjoy it as a not-so-guilty pleasure!

Makes 1 loaf

I recipe Master Sweet Loaf (page 124)

FILLING:

⅓ cup (3 ounces) smooth peanut butter

¼ cup (2 ounces) jam, like raspberry
(avoid preserves or a jam with lots of fruit chunks)

GLAZE:

½ cup (2¼ ounces) confectioners' sugar

I tablespoon buttermilk

2 tablespoons finely chopped, lightly salted peanuts

Proceed with the recipe for the Master Sweet Loaf through the first rise. Fold the dough over, once in each direction, to release the gases. Roll the dough out to approximately 11 x 8 inches.

Put the peanut butter and jam into two separate bowls. The peanut butter may be sticky, and it may be necessary to warm it slightly in the microwave. Heating it will make it more liquid. On the long side of the dough, and starting ¼ inch in, spread some of the peanut butter in a line, roughly 1¼ inches wide. Next to the line of peanut butter, make another line of equal proportions with the jam. Repeat the process so there are two lines of jam and three lines of peanut butter, ending with the peanut butter. Roll the dough tightly to form a cylinder. Pinch the final seam of dough to the cylinder 11 inches long, closing the roll. Tuck the ends under, and place it in a loaf pan.

Cover the pan with plastic wrap, and let the loaf rise for 1 to 1½ hours, or until doubled in bulk. It is fine if the bread is not quite cresting the lip of the pan before baking. Because of the swirled interior, you will want a more contained loaf of bread.

Arrange the oven rack in the middle of the oven, and fifteen minutes prior to baking, preheat to 350°F.

Remove the plastic wrap, and place the pan in the center of the oven and bake for approximately 35 to 40 minutes, rotating once at the halfway point.

Remove the loaf from the oven, and set it on a cooling rack for approximately 5 minutes. Release the loaf from its pan, and allow it to cool to room temperature.

Make the glaze. In a small bowl, mix together the confectioners' sugar and the buttermilk. The glaze should be fluid and lump-free. Set a piece of wax paper underneath the cooling rack to catch any overflow. Pour the glaze over the top of the bread, and then sprinkle with the peanuts. Allow it to harden for 1 hour, and then enjoy.

Swirled Chocolate Cherry Bread

WHY ARE THERE NO CHOCOLATE BREADS? THIS QUESTION PLAGUED ME. NOT WHITE BREAD STUDDED with chocolate—though that is delicious—but a genuine dark loaf that is made with chocolate. Well, I was going to try to remedy this tragedy, and here it is—one scrumptious bread!

Adding chocolate can be a bit of a sticky situation—or a dry one, as it turned out to be. Melted chocolate is not a viable option, because it changes the proportion of liquid and fat in dough. Unsweetened cocoa powder is the best solution. It's a powder, resembling flour, but while it can be kneaded into the dough, it has no glutens itself—so it can get stiff, creating a coarse bread. But cocoa does have flavor, and flavor is really what I was looking for.

This recipe solves the problem of a dry chocolate dough by twisting it with a rich, eggy, and sumptuous vanilla dough. The two doughs mingle perfectly together and make a stunning, decorative loaf of bread. Studded with dried cherries, sprinkled with sanding sugar, and finally drizzled with a sweet glaze, this bread is definitely something to see, but it's something to eat, as well! It is not overwhelmingly sweet; the chocolate is in its essence, complemented tastily by the vanilla-scented dough. Sliced thickly and enjoyed on its own, or adorned with a smear of cream cheese, keep one loaf for yourself, and give the other to a very good friend.

Makes 2 loaves

¼ cup warm water (100° to 115°F)

3 teaspoons dry yeast

Pinch of sugar

1 cup whole milk, at room temperature

4 tablespoons (2 ounces) unsalted butter,
at room temperature, plus 1 tablespoon, melted

½ cup (3½ ounces) sugar

2 eggs

2 teaspoons vanilla extract

1½ teaspoons kosher salt

3½ to 4 cups (1 pound, 1½ ounces to 1 pound, 4 ounces)
all-purpose flour

½ cup (2½ ounces) dried cherries, chopped

¼ cup (¾ ounce) unsweetened cocoa powder

1 egg

2 teaspoons sanding sugar, or turbinado sugar

GLAZE:

½ cup (2¼ ounces) confectioners' sugar

½ teaspoon vanilla

3 to 4 teaspoons whole milk

In a small bowl or glass, mix the water, yeast, and sugar together. Allow the mixture to bloom. It should become bubbly and smell yeasty, about 10 minutes.

In the bowl of a stand mixer fitted with the paddle attachment, add the milk, butter, sugar, eggs, vanilla, salt, and 2 cups (10 ounces) of flour. At low speed, mix until just combined. Add the yeast mixture, and mix briefly. Add another ½ cup (2½ ounces) of flour, and continue to mix at low speed until the mixture becomes web-like and more difficult to mix with the paddle attachment.

Remove the paddle and attach the dough hook. With the mixer on low speed, begin kneading with the dough hook, adding additional flour in ¼- to ½-cup increments. The dough will become a more cohesive mass and more elastic. Add the cherries, and continue to mix. It is important to watch the dough during this process. Stop the kneading process in the machine when the dough is almost too tacky and could easily take more kneading and more flour. You will have added approximately ½ cup (2½ ounces) of flour, approximately 3 to 3½ cups (17.5 ounces to a pound), total. More flour will added by hand. Empty the dough out onto a well-floured work surface, and divide it in half.

Take one portion of the dough and sprinkle the cocoa powder over it. Begin kneading it by hand. The dough will become more difficult to work with as the cocoa is more evenly worked throughout. Keep kneading until the dough is a sandy brown color, and no streaks of cocoa remain. This will take approximately 3 minutes. Put the dough into a large bowl, and place a piece of plastic wrap on the surface. Clean the work surface well; you don't want any remnants of chocolate dough in the plain bread.

Knead the plain bread, adding any additional flour in order to make it smooth and less tacky. This can take up to ½ cup (2½ ounces) of flour. Put the dough into a large bowl, and place a piece of plastic wrap on the surface.

Place both bowls in a warm spot, and let the doughs rise approximately 2 hours, or until doubled in bulk. It is fine if the two doughs have not risen at the same speed. You are mainly looking at the rising time of the plain dough.

Brush two loaf pans with the melted butter.

Pull back the plastic wrap, and empty the doughs out onto a well-floured surface. Fold the first dough over, once in each direction, to release the gases. Repeat with other dough. Divide the white dough in half, and roll each portion into a cylinder, about 16 inches in length. Cover with a towel or plastic wrap while you work on the chocolate roll. Divide the chocolate dough in half, and roll each portion into a cylinder, about 16 inches in length.

Take two rolls, one white and the other chocolate, and lay them side by side. Pinch the two doughs together firmly, and then twist the doughs around each other. Pinch the ends firmly closed. The twisted dough should be about 10 inches in length. Gently pick up the twisted dough, and place it snugly into a prepared loaf pan. Repeat with the second set of rolls.

Cover the pans with plastic wrap, and let the loaves rise for 1 to 1$^1/_2$ hours, or until doubled in bulk. It is fine if the bread is not quite cresting the lip of the pan before baking.

Arrange the oven rack in the middle of the oven, and fifteen minutes prior to baking, preheat to 350°F.

Beat the egg and 1 tablespoon water together. Remove the plastic wrap, and paint egg wash onto the surface of each loaf. Generously sprinkle the sanding sugar over the loaves.

Place the pans in the center of the oven, and bake for approximately 35 to 40 minutes, rotating once at the halfway point.

Remove the loaves from the oven, and set them on a cooling rack for approximately 5 minutes. Release the loaves from their pans, and allow them to cool to room temperature.

To make the glaze, in a small bowl, add the confectioner's sugar and vanilla. Add the milk, one teaspoonful at a time, until a smooth glaze is formed. With a spoon, lightly drizzle the glaze back and forth across the surface of the breads. Allow it to set one hour before eating; the glaze will harden substantially.

QUICKBREADS

JUST WHAT IS A QUICKBREAD? IT'S WHAT IT SOUNDS LIKE—A BREAD THAT doesn't take the same time to proof as a yeast bread. Leavened with baking soda or baking powder (more on the differences between the two on page 147), a quickbread can be a delectable component to any meal. In the South, biscuits (page 144) are a staple during meals. In the North, there is Boston Brown Bread (page 140), rich with molasses and studded with raisins. Every region has their answer to the age-old problem of needing to feed your family something hearty in a relatively short amount of time. In this chapter, you can tour the regions and pick a bread for yourself.

Boston Brown Bread

TODAY, FINDING AN ACTUAL METAL COFFEE CAN TO BAKE THIS BREAD IN IS PROBABLY THE MOST challenging aspect of this recipe, but in Colonial times, this recipe was a challenge for substitution's sake. White flour was at a premium for early New Englanders. Often, it was blended with other, more plentiful flours for baking. Settlers made bread from the abundance of rye flour and cornmeal—which the Native Americans introduced to them. These new flours were coarser and heavier than European flours, but they were also rich and sustaining. Bread was often baked in a fireplace, but the temperature could be difficult to regulate. Therefore, alternatives such as steaming were routinely favored.

Steaming for a long duration ensures that all of the ingredients meld nicely, allowing the cornmeal to soften and the rye flour to plump and reconstitute. Sweetened with molasses (another abundant Colonial ingredient) and speckled with raisins, Boston Brown Bread is dark and delicately sweet. It is wonderful the day it is baked, but it's also excellent the next day, fried crisply in butter.

In this recipe, I bake the bread in the oven, but do so in a water bath. This creates the same steamy environment early settlers might have had, but allows you to simply pop the bread in the oven and leave it, rather than continually checking it to make sure the water has not cooked out of the pot.

Makes 1 loaf

I tablespoon (½ ounce) unsalted butter, melted

½ cup (2½ ounces) rye flour

¼ cup (1¼ ounces) whole wheat flour

¼ cup (1¼ ounces) all-purpose flour

½ cup (2½ ounces) cornmeal

I teaspoon baking powder

¼ teaspoon baking soda

½ teaspoon kosher salt

⅓ cup molasses

I cup buttermilk

½ cup (2½ ounces) raisins

Preheat oven to 325°F. Grease a 1-pound, metal coffee can with the melted butter, and set aside.

In a medium-size bowl, whisk the flours and the cornmeal together. Mix in the baking powder, baking soda, and salt. Stir in the molasses and buttermilk until combined. Fold in the raisins.

Pour the batter into the prepared coffee can. It should be about ⅔ full. Cover the top with a piece of lightly greased foil. Secure the foil with kitchen twine or a rubber band.

Place the can in a baking dish. Pour boiling water into the dish so it comes halfway up the side of the can. Bake for 2 hours, checking the water level at 1 hour. A skewer will come out clean when the bread is finished baking. Remove the foil cover, and let cool in the can for 1 hour before unmolding.

Graham Puffs

THE PEERLESS COOK-BOOK WAS A GENERAL GUIDE FOR THE NINETEENTH-CENTURY HOUSEWIFE BY MRS. D.A. Lincoln, containing "valuable receipts for cooking." This slim, little volume is "compact and practical," with recipes for making hop yeast, a variety of gems (the common name for a muffin in the 1800s), and this delightful recipe for Graham Puffs—a wheaty popover. While the recipe does set apart a list of all the ingredients (many recipes at this time contained no lists, and measurements were just assumed), the directions were rather vague. I toyed with the recipe some, and came up with this modern take on a classic.

Puffs, or popovers, were quite common in nineteenth century America. They were eaten for breakfast or enjoyed as a snack with tea or coffee. There are many recipes calling for plain flour and a varying number of eggs. Some are sweetened; some are not. But this recipe, with the inclusion of graham flour, really cannot be beat. I have sweetened these puffs slightly with sugar, but the sweet wheat flavor found in the graham flour lends a richness all its own. It's important that these puffs be eaten immediately—they wait for no one. They will balloon and color beautifully while baking, but they will begin to deflate as soon as they are taken from the oven.

One hint: In addition to buttering the insides of the muffin pans, spread a little melted butter around the rim as well. This will make extracting the puffs much easier. These puffs are delicious with a bit of jam spread on them, but they are equally wonderful dipped in pure maple syrup!

Makes 9 to 12 puffs,
depending on the muffin tin

I cup whole milk

3 eggs

3 tablespoons (1½ ounces) unsalted butter,
melted and divided

I tablespoon sugar

½ teaspoon kosher salt

½ cup (2½ ounces) all-purpose flour

½ cup (2½ ounces) graham flour

It is best to blend this batter, so I suggest assembling it in a blender, or using a quart measuring cup with an immersion blender.

Blend the milk, eggs, 2 tablespoons melted butter, sugar, and salt together. When the mixture is thoroughly combined, sift in both of the flours. Blend again for about 30 seconds. The batter will be very loose and smooth. Let the batter rest for 15 minutes.

Preheat oven to 400°F. With a pastry brush, coat the insides and top of a muffin tin well with the remainder of the melted butter.

After 15 minutes have passed, carefully pour the batter about $\frac{2}{3}$ full into the cups of the muffin tin. Bake for 30 to 35 minutes. Puffs will have inflated and be golden-brown. Remove them from the oven; they may need assistance being released from the muffin tin. If so, extract them with an off-set spatula, and then serve immediately.

Southern-Style Biscuits

LONG BEFORE THERE WERE REFRIGERATED CYLINDERS OF MEDIOCRE BISCUIT DOUGH AT EVERY SUPER-market waiting to be popped from their container and tossed into the oven, there were fresh, homebaked biscuits. In the South, each woman has her own special recipe, her own process, and her own lore surrounding the biscuit. Do you use vegetable shortening or butter; do you roll out the dough or pat it gently with your hands? What about baking powder—how many tablespoons; do you knead it or hardly touch the dough? With so much mythologizing, it's no wonder that Americans have settled on the mediocrity of a convenience food just to avoid treading on an adamant baker's toes!

While I appreciate a tale as much as the next woman, I also believe in *de*-mystifying processes, showing every person (Southern or otherwise) that getting a plate full of steaming biscuits on the table is an achievable goal. So here are a few helpful hints to guide you:

• Aerate your dry ingredients; you want feather-weight biscuits. By whisking the flour mixture, you are incorporating air, making it as light and lump-free as possible.

• This recipe uses both baking powder and baking soda as leaveners. This ensures an adequate rise. Because of the acidity of the buttermilk (the wet ingredient), the addition of baking soda is needed.

• It is important that all of the fats used are cold. You don't want them to completely dissolve, melting as you are making the dough. Discrete layers of fat in the biscuit dough equals layers in the baked biscuit.

- I use equal amounts of cold butter and cold vegetable shortening in my biscuits. The butter adds flavor and tenderness, and the shortening adds lightness and flakiness.

- Don't overwork the ingredients. The fats should be mixed in quickly. It is fine if there is some disparity in size when you are incorporating the fats into the flour. In fact, it is preferable. This will make a supremely light and flaky biscuit.

- Add the buttermilk into the dry ingredients all at once, and don't overmix! You want the dough to just hold together.

- Don't knead the dough. When you are making biscuits, it is different from making yeast breads. Here, you don't want gluten development, so kneading is unnecessary.

- Leave the rolling pin in the drawer. Use the heel of your hand to pat out the dough.

- Using a rolling pin compresses the ingredients, and you risk the dough sticking to the rolling pin.

- Folding the dough will create flaky layers in the baked biscuit.

- Bake the biscuits in a hot oven; 450°F is best. This will make a biscuit that is golden on the outside while maintaining a moist interior.

- If a soft-sided biscuit is what you desire, bake the biscuits close together. If you desire crusty sides, bake 1 inch apart.

Makes 9 to 12 biscuits
(recipe can easily be doubled)

2 cups (10 ounces) all-purpose flour

1 tablespoon baking powder

¼ teaspoon baking soda

¾ teaspoon kosher salt

3 tablespoons (1½ ounces) unsalted butter, chilled,
cut into ½-inch cubes

3 tablespoons (1¼ ounces) vegetable shortening, chilled,
cut into ½-inch cubes

1 cup buttermilk

Preheat oven to 450°F.

In a medium-size bowl, whisk the flour, baking powder, baking soda, and salt together to blend. The mixture should be light and free of lumps.

Add the butter and the shortening, and toss gently to coat. With your fingertips, work the fats into the flour mixture, rubbing the larger pieces between your fingers until they are pea-size.

Add the buttermilk all at once. With a wooden spoon or rubber spatula, mix the ingredients until they're just blended and coming together to form a dough. Do not overmix.

Empty the dough onto a clean, well-floured work surface. Gently pat the dough out into a rectangle approximately 12 x 8 inches. Lightly flour the surface. Fold the dough into thirds, as if you are folding a letter. Scrape the folded dough from the work surface; if necessary, flour the surface again. Once more, pat the dough into a rectangle, flour lightly, and fold into thirds. Finally, pat the dough out to a thickness of approximately 1 inch.

With a well-floured 2- or 2½-inch round biscuit cutter, cut biscuits out, and place them on a baking sheet. You may reshape biscuits from the scraps, but they will not rise as high as the first cutting.

Bake for 12 to 15 minutes, or until the biscuits are a light, golden brown. If you would like, biscuits can be brushed with an additional coating of melted butter. Serve immediately. Biscuits are best eaten the same day that they are baked, but any leftovers can be eaten warm the next day. Simply reheat them in a low 300° oven for 5 minutes.

The Difference Between Baking Soda and Baking Powder

I f you bake at all, you most likely have these two ingredients in your pantry. And if you ever bake from a cookbook, then you carefully follow directions, and use one, the other, or both, when instructed. But have you ever truly understood the difference between baking soda and baking powder? These two ingredients are chemical leaveners—meaning they give rise to your baked goods. They make your biscuits light and fluffy and prevent your quickbreads from turning to leaden bricks. These items are like yeast, but quicker; they incorporate air into what you bake.

Baking soda is the faster and stronger of these two leaveners—but it needs an additional, acidic ingredient in order to activate. That's why you'll often see baking soda included in recipes with buttermilk or lemon juice. But there are other ingredients, such as molasses, cocoa, and even honey, that you might not think of as acidic, but in fact are. When baking soda, or sodium bicarbonate, as it is scientifically known, mingles with wet, acidic ingredients, it begins to produce sodium carbonate, which produce those tiny, hardworking bubbles that make your baked goods fluffy and light. The only problem is, sodium carbonate can have an unpleasant, metallic aftertaste, so baking soda should be used in moderation.

Baking powder is the clumpier and the starchier of the two, and it actually contains baking soda. This powder is made of sodium bicarbonate (baking soda), cream of tartar, to acidify, and a bit of cornstarch (to wick away moisture). Today, most baking powders are double-acting—meaning they will continue to be active while setting or baking for a longer period of time. Baking powder can also withstand high heat.

So what do you need to know about these two products to help you in your baking endeavors? Baking soda is like the sports car, and baking powder is the family sedan. Baking soda is powerful and strong when used correctly, and given the right amount of fuel (acidic ingredients), it will work like a dream. Baking powder is more deliberate—slow and steady wins the race. While it is possible to substitute baking powder for baking soda, this rule doesn't go both ways. Recipes with long cooking times won't do well with baking soda alone; they require the long fuel of baking powder, not simply the burst of baking soda.

Pinwheel Biscuits

AS THE BAKERS FROM OUR PAST KNEW ONLY TOO WELL, THERE IS MORE TO BE BAKED WITH BISCUIT dough than biscuits alone. It is much quicker to mix up a batch of biscuit dough than it is to proof, rise, and then bake a batch of sweet rolls, and they can be equally as delicious. In my vintage cookbooks, I often find recipes for pinwheel biscuits—jam rolled inside biscuit dough, sliced to resemble a cinnamon roll, and baked to a golden brown. Some of these recipes use chopped dried fruit, others a little cinnamon and sugar; some glazed, others leave the biscuits plain. Brilliant—a warm roll, without much work! Once I got to thinking about this delicious combination, my mind reeled. You could fill them with cheese, or with wilted spinach for a savory brunch. What about a sticky bun biscuit? Once you get to thinking, I guarantee, you just won't quit!

This recipe is for the simplest and most traditional of pinwheel biscuits. Filled with jam and drizzled with a buttermilk glaze, this recipe is just to get you started on your pinwheel experimentation. Just remember, it's important not to overfill the biscuits, or you will end up with a sticky mess.

Makes 9 rolls

1 recipe Southern-Style Biscuits (page 144)

3 tablespoons raspberry jam,
or another type of relatively smooth jam

GLAZE:

⅓ cup (1½ ounces) confectioners' sugar

1 tablespoon buttermilk

Preheat oven to 450°F. Butter an 8-inch square cooking pan, or liberally coat it with cooking spray. Set aside.

Follow the Southern-Style Biscuit recipe through the second round of folding and patting out the dough. Pat the dough out to approximately 10 x 8 inches. Spread the jam over the surface, leaving ½ inch of space on the longer sides of the dough. Roll it tightly to form a cylinder 10 inches long. Pinch the final seam of dough to the cylinder, closing the roll. Gently roll the cylinder back and forth to make sure that it is amply secure and moves easily from the counter.

With a sharp knife, cut the dough into 9 equal pieces, a little over 1 inch long. Place each biscuit in the pan; they will fit fairly snugly. Bake for about 14 to 17 minutes, or until golden brown on top. Remove the pan from the oven, and let them cool slightly.

In a small bowl, whisk the confectioners' sugar with the buttermilk until smooth. The glaze will still be fairly runny. Drizzle the glaze over the rolls. Enjoy them while still warm.

Sweet Potato Biscuits

THESE BISCUITS ARE LIKE THE SOUTHERN-STYLE BISCUITS (PAGE 144), BUT MORE SUBSTANTIAL. STUR-dier, creamier, a tad sweeter—Sweet Potato Biscuits are a welcome alternative. They have a flavor all their own due to the addition of this tuber, making them an ideal breakfast treat with butter and jam, or a sumptuous luncheon bread split and filled with country ham. These biscuits have added starch, so they won't rise quite as high as the Southern-Style Biscuit, but they're still light as can be!

Makes 9 to 12 biscuits
(recipe can be easily doubled)

1½ cups (7½ ounces) all-purpose flour

¾ cup (about 8 or 10 ounces) cooked, riced,
or well-mashed sweet potato [see Note]

1 tablespoon baking powder

¼ teaspoon baking soda

2 teaspoons sugar

¾ teaspoon kosher salt

3 tablespoons (1½ ounces) unsalted butter,
chilled, cut into ½-inch cubes

3 tablespoons (1¼ ounces) vegetable shortening,
chilled, cut into ½-inch cubes

⅓ cup buttermilk

Preheat the oven to 450°F.

In a medium-size bowl, whisk the flour, sweet potato, baking powder, baking soda, sugar, and salt together to blend. This will coat the sweet potato in flour, and ensures that the mixture is free of lumps.

Add the butter and the shortening, and toss gently to coat. With your fingertips, work the fats into the flour mixture, rubbing the larger pieces between you fingers until they are pea-size.

Add the buttermilk all at once. With a wooden spoon or rubber spatula, mix until just blended and coming together to form a dough.

Empty the dough onto a clean, well-floured surface. Gently pat the dough out into a rectangle approximately 12 x 8 inches. Lightly flour the surface. Fold the dough into thirds, as if you are folding a letter. Scrape the folded dough from the work surface; if necessary, flour the surface again. Once more, pat the dough into a rectangle, flour lightly, and fold into thirds. Finally, pat the dough out to a thickness of approximately 1 inch.

With a well-floured 2- or 2 1/2-inch round biscuit cutter, cut the biscuits out, and place them on a baking sheet. You may reshape biscuits from the scraps, but they will not rise as high as the first cutting.

Bake for 12 to 15 minutes, or until biscuits are a light, golden brown. If you would like, biscuits can be brushed with an additional coating of melted butter. Serve immediately. Biscuits are best eaten the day that they are baked, but any leftovers can be eaten warm the next day. Simply reheat them in a 300°F oven for 5 minutes.

NOTE: For this recipe, the best method of cooking a sweet potato is baking. If you were to boil them, the sweet potato would absorb excess moisture. To bake, simply prick the surface of the skin with a fork, and bake in a preheated 400°F oven, on a sheet of foil, for approximately 45 minutes.

I prefer a ricer to mash my sweet potatoes. It makes a fine, even mash. If you don't have a ricer, you can mash the potatoes finely with a fork. The sweet potato mash should be entirely cool before proceeding with the recipe. This step can be done the day before and stored in the refrigerator.

Vermont Graham Bread

SYLVESTER GRAHAM COULD BE CONSIDERED ONE OF AMERICA'S EARLY HEALTH FANATICS. THE OWNER of a chain of "health" hotels, he was abstemious and advised against alcohol, caffeine, salt, and overeating. As a way of diverting people from eating white flour, a flour he despised due to its lack of nutrients, he invented Graham flour—a rich, whole wheat flour. Graham flour takes advantage of milling the entire wheat berry. The endosperm is finely ground, and then the bran and the germ are coarsely ground and added back to the flour. The final product is a coarser grind than even whole wheat flour. This flour has a nutty punch and a gentle sweetness.

In Vermont, they up the flavor ante by using their favorite local sweetener—pure maple syrup. This simple quickbread also contains a handful of raisins for a bit of chewiness, as well as sweetness. The bread is dense and wholesome—homey. Thrown together in a matter of moments, it can be enjoyed any time of day, but it is really best served while still warm and adorned with salted butter. An addition of which Sylvester Graham would surely not approve!

Makes 1 loaf

1½ cups (7½ ounces) graham flour

1 cup (5 ounces) all-purpose flour

1½ teaspoons baking soda

¼ teaspoon ground nutmeg

½ teaspoon kosher salt

⅓ cup (2 ounces) brown sugar, packed

¼ cup pure maple syrup

1 egg

1 cup buttermilk

½ cup (2½ ounces) raisins

Preheat oven to 350°F. Butter a standard loaf pan, or lightly coat it with cooking spray.

In a large bowl, whisk the flours, baking soda, nutmeg, and salt together. Set aside. In a medium-size bowl, whisk the brown sugar, maple syrup, egg, and buttermilk together until well blended. All at once, add the wet ingredients to the dry ingredients, mixing until just combined. Fold in the raisins.

Pour the batter into the prepared loaf pan, smoothing the top. Bake for 45 to 50 minutes, or until the bread is lightly browned, and a toothpick inserted in the center of the loaf comes out clean. Cool in the pan for 10 minutes, then unmold. The bread can be sliced and eaten while still warm.

NOTE: Graham flour can be found in health food stores and some grocery stores. Bob's Red Mill, as well as Hodgson Mills, make great graham flours. If you are having trouble finding it, you can substitute whole wheat flour, though the bread will not have the same nuttiness or flavor.

Browned Butter Banana Bread

THERE ARE SO MANY BANANA BREAD RECIPES OUT THERE, IT SEEMS LIKE YOU COULD PICK A NEW ONE to try every day for a year, and you would just begin to scratch the surface of all of the options. Some have nuts, some are spiced, a few have chocolate chips; some are made with butter, others oils, some have just a smidge of banana, and others are overflowing with the fruit.

Well, here is another banana bread to add to your repertoire, and this has one special ingredient in it—browned butter. What was once something *haute cuisine* has now become *de rigueur*. Browned butter is appearing in dishes both savory and sweet, and I must say, it is delectable in this quickbread. The bread itself is flavored with just bananas, so as not to compete with the browned butter, but it also has a lightly spiced crumb topping, a welcome addition to this moist bread.

Makes 1 loaf

8 tablespoons (4 ounces) unsalted butter

2 cups (10 ounces) all-purpose flour

2 teaspoons baking powder

½ teaspoon kosher salt

¾ cup (4½ ounces) brown sugar, packed

2 eggs

1 cup very ripe bananas, mashed, about 3 bananas

⅓ cup milk

1 teaspoon vanilla extract

TOPPING:

¼ cup (1¼ ounces) all-purpose flour

2 tablespoons sugar

2 tablespoons brown sugar, packed

¼ teaspoon cinnamon

Pinch of kosher salt

2 tablespoons (1 ounce) unsalted butter, chilled, cut into ½-inch cubes

Preheat oven to 350°F. Butter a standard loaf pan, or lightly coat it with cooking spray.

In a medium-size stainless steel or other light-colored saucepan (you'll need to really see the color of the butter as it cooks) over medium heat, melt the butter. Once melted, the butter will begin to foam; as this subsides, continue to cook, swirling the pan, keeping a close eye on its contents. The butter will begin to color and become highly aromatic. Watch it closely. When it turns a light, nut-brown color, immediately take it off the heat. This should take about 5 minutes. Pour the butter into a separate bowl to ensure that it stops cooking. Set aside to cool.

Make the topping. In a separate bowl, combine the flour, sugar, brown sugar, cinnamon, and salt. Add the butter, and use your fingers to work it into the dry mixture until the topping resembles large crumbs. Set aside.

In a medium-size bowl, whisk the flour, baking powder, and salt together. In the bowl of a stand mixer, or with a hand mixer, beat the brown sugar and the browned butter together until light and fluffy. One at a time, add the eggs. Add the banana, milk, and vanilla, beating until thoroughly combined. Add the flour mixture all at once, and mix by hand until just combined.

Pour the batter into the loaf pan. Sprinkle the topping evenly over the banana bread batter.

Bake for approximately 1 hour, or until a toothpick inserted in the center of the loaf comes out clean. Cool the loaf in the pan for 15 to 20 minutes, then unmold and cool completely before enjoying.

Savannah Banana Bread

ELVIS PRESLEY MAY HAVE LOVED THE COMBINATION OF PEANUT BUTTER AND BANANA (WITH THE addition of bacon, of course), but apparently he wasn't the only Southerner to fancy the richness of peanut butter combined with the sweet flavor of ripe bananas. In Georgia, this is marriage made in quickbread heaven.

During my research for this book, I saw this listed as both Georgia Banana Bread and Savannah Banana Bread, but I prefer the rhyming name. This version, adapted from *The Ladies Aid Cookbook* by Beatrice Vaughan, enlisted members from ladies auxiliary groups from around the country to donate homestyle recipes that women made for their families. I think it strikes just the right balance of salty and sweet, moist and decadent. Wrapped in plastic and left at room temperature, this bread stays fresh for quite a few days.

Makes 1 loaf

4 tablespoons (2 ounces) unsalted butter,
at room temperature

¾ cup (7½ ounces) chunky peanut butter,
not the natural kind

1 cup (7 ounces) sugar

2 eggs

1 teaspoon vanilla extract

1¾ cups (8¾ ounces) all-purpose flour

2 teaspoons baking powder

¼ teaspoon baking soda

½ teaspoon kosher salt

1 cup very ripe bananas, mashed, about 3 bananas

1 tablespoon sanding
or turbinado sugar, optional

Preheat oven to 350°F. Butter a standard loaf pan, or lightly coat it with cooking spray.

In the bowl of a stand mixer, cream the butter and the peanut butter together until smooth. Blend in the sugar, eggs, and vanilla thoroughly. In a separate, medium-sized bowl, whisk the flour, baking powder, baking soda, and salt together. In four parts, add the flour mixture, alternating with banana, ending with the banana, until just incorporated.

Pour the batter into the prepared loaf pan, smoothing the top. If using, sprinkle with the sanding or turbinado sugar. Bake for approximately 1 hour, or until the bread is golden brown and a toothpick inserted in the center of the loaf comes out clean. Cool in the pan for 10 minutes, then unmold. The bread can be sliced and eaten while still warm.

FREEZING RIPE BANANAS

In my childhood home, we seemed to have a lot of bananas that were past their prime. My mom called these "tired bananas"—which always made me think of a bunch of these liver-spotted bananas in flannel pajamas, getting ready to turn in for the night.

Sometimes my mom was too busy, or the baking bug just didn't strike, and those tired bananas went straight into the trashcan. I wish that we had known about freezing those black bananas when I was a kid. Today, at my house, you will find anywhere from three to eight tired bananas taking a chilly doze. Those blackened, mushy pieces of fruit freeze beautifully, peel and all. There they can stay for a few months until you are ready to bake something delicious. Simply defrost them completely, peel and discard the skin, and then bake to your heart's content!

Bishop's Bread

AN AMERICAN FRUIT BREAD, "BISHOP'S BREAD" IS THOUGHT TO HAVE BEEN COINED IN THE NINETEENTH century when clergymen would visit settlers and were often fed a little something sweet to eat with a cup of coffee or tea. It has dried or candied fruit in it, making this bread often seem like a fruitcake. But it can also be studded with nuts, swirled with chocolate, and spiced with cinnamon. Because of its "fruitcake" nature, nowadays it is often thought of as a holiday treat, but I find that the ease of mixing up this quickbread makes it a wonderful treat to have year-round.

In this recipe I use it all—in moderation. A bit of bittersweet chocolate, some toasted slivered almonds, and a serving of dried cherries or cranberries make this bread a restrained treat. I favor baking with dried rather than candied fruit—I want the pure flavor of the berry. And by reconstituting the fruit, the berries plump up, making this simple bread sumptuous.

Makes 1 loaf

½ cup (2 ounces) slivered almonds

½ cup (2½ ounces) dried cherries or cranberries

I cup boiling water

8 tablespoons (4 ounces) unsalted butter,
at room temperature

I cup (6 ounces) brown sugar, packed

2 eggs

I cup buttermilk

½ teaspoon almond extract

2 cups (10 ounces) all-purpose flour

1½ teaspoons baking powder

½ teaspoon baking soda

½ teaspoon kosher salt

½ cup (2 ounces) bittersweet chocolate chunks

Preheat oven to 325°F. Place the almonds on a small baking pan and roast for 15 to 18 minutes, or until toasty and fragrant. Remove the almonds from the oven, let them cool, and set them aside. Pour boiling water over the cherries and soak for 15 to 30 minutes. Drain well, and set aside.

Turn the oven up to 350°F. Butter a standard loaf pan, or lightly coat it with cooking spray.

In the bowl of stand mixer, cream the butter and the brown sugar together until light and fluffy, about 2 minutes. One at a time, add the eggs, beating until combined. Mix in the buttermilk and the almond extract. In a separate, medium-size bowl, whisk the flour, baking powder, baking soda, and salt together. Slowly combine the dry ingredients into the wet ingredients, and mix until just combined. Fold in the almonds, berries, and chocolate chunks.

Pour the batter into the prepared loaf pan, smoothing the top. Bake for approximately 1 hour to 1 hour 15 minutes, or until the bread is golden brown, and a toothpick inserted in the center of the loaf comes out clean. Cool in the pan for 10 minutes, then unmold. The bread can be sliced and eaten while still warm.

Peanut Butter-Bacon Bread

IT SEEMS THAT BACON HAS BEEN TRENDING FOR YEARS NOW—DECADES EVEN. THIS SALTY, SMOKY breakfast meat is not simply popular with hipsters and breakfast lovers; just ask Helen Corbitt. Best known for her work as Director of Food Services for Neiman-Marcus department stores during the 1950s, Ms. Corbitt had a penchant for interesting yet delicious food combinations. This quickbread is just one of those treats. In her 1957 book, *Helen Corbitt's Cookbook*, Ms. Corbitt claims this bread is "nice for morning entertaining," but I would say it's a treat any time of the day.

The richness of the peanut butter and the salinity of the bacon makes for a scrumptious combination. Yes, the bread contains crispy, fried bacon bits, but this contributes to an overall smoky effect in the bread, not just a bacon-y one. I have updated this recipe by using crunchy peanut butter for added textural dimension, a bit of brown sugar as well as granulated sugar for depth, and just a hint of black pepper. Try to use an artisanal, thick-cut bacon; the meatiness plays off the pepper deliciously.

Makes 1 loaf

4 tablespoons (2 ounces) unsalted butter,
at room temperature

½ cup (3½ ounces) sugar

½ cup (3 ounces) brown sugar, packed

1 cup (10½ ounces) crunchy peanut butter

1 cup whole milk

1 egg

2 cups (10 ounces) flour

3 teaspoons baking powder

½ teaspoon kosher salt

¼ teaspoon freshly ground black pepper

½ cup (2½ ounces) lightly salted peanuts, coarsely chopped

½ pound thick-cut bacon (about 6 slices) crisply cooked,
drained, and crumbled

1 tablespoon sanding or turbinando sugar

Preheat oven to 350°F. Butter a standard loaf pan, or lightly coat it with cooking spray.

In a large mixing bowl, cream the butter, sugar, brown sugar, and peanut butter together until light and fluffy. Add the milk and egg, and continue to mix until just blended.

In a separate bowl, whisk the flour, baking powder, salt, and pepper together. In two parts, add to the peanut butter mixture, and mix until well-incorporated. Fold in the chopped nuts and the bacon.

Pour the batter into the prepared loaf pan, spreading evenly. The batter will fill the pan about ¾ of the way. This is fine, as the bread is rather dense and will not rise substantially. Sprinkle with sanding or turbinado sugar. Bake for 1 hour, or until a toothpick inserted in the center comes out clean. Cool in the pan for 10 minutes, and then remove the loaf from the pan and continue to cool to room temperature on a wire rack.

CORNBREAD

CORN WAS A FOOD OF THE NEW WORLD, AND IT SEEMS THAT SETTLERS OF the North, South, East, and West began incorporating cornmeal into their baking from the beginning. Some cornbreads are dry and salty; others are cakey and sweet. They are accompaniments; they act as ballasts sopping up savory flavors from the meal; they are as good at breakfast as they are a midday snack. Here is just a sampling of some of the cornbreads that I have enjoyed baking. Some are sweet, others savory—pick the one that best complements your meal.

Southern-Style Cornbread

THEY MAY LIKE THEIR CAKES PILED HIGH WITH FROSTING, THE MERINGUES ON THEIR PIES BILLOWY AND sweet, and their morning rolls sweet as the day is long, but when it comes to cornbread south of the Mason-Dixon line, no sugar is ever wanted! In the South, the cornbread is rather ascetic. This bread is meant to be enjoyed with a meal; it's a component, not the shining star. Meant to sop up sauces from the entrée, or to even to be crumbled atop a dish of greens, Southern-style cornbread understands its place as an *accoutrement*.

Being from the North myself, this style of cornbread was novel to me, but knowing just how Southerners respect food traditions, I didn't want to mess up this recipe! I went to the source and enlisted help from a proper Southern gentleman. In the foothills of Rising Fawn, Georgia lives Michael Thompson, a friend of a friend, and this is his family recipe. It's delicious, moist (despite the abundance of cornmeal), light, and chock full of true corn flavor. Michael says it *must* be baked in a cast-iron skillet. And I agree. The pan should be coated with a film of bacon grease—both for flavor and its non-stick properties. Michael also suggests pouring the batter into the pan in a zig-zag pattern. He says this further prevents sticking, and this Northern girl does as she's told . . . at least when it comes to cornbread.

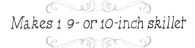

Makes 1 9- or 10-inch skillet

1 tablespoon bacon grease

1½ cups (7½ ounces) fine-grained cornmeal

⅓ cup (1⅔ ounces) all-purpose flour

4 teaspoons baking powder

1 teaspoon baking soda

1 teaspoon kosher salt

2 eggs

1½ cups buttermilk, scant

Put the bacon grease in a cast-iron skillet; it is unnecessary to melt it. Place the skillet, with the grease, in the center rack of the oven, and then preheat both to 425°F.

In a medium-size bowl, whisk the cornmeal, flour, baking powder, baking soda, and salt together until free of lumps. Set aside.

In a pint-size measuring cup, beat the eggs. Add the buttermilk, measuring to just slightly less than 2 cups. This should take approximately 1½ cups of buttermilk. Beat the liquid measurements until combined.

All at once, pour the wet ingredients into the dry ingredients. Mix until combined; the batter should still have lumps, but be thoroughly combined.

Remove the pan from the oven. Swirl the bacon grease around, amply coating the pan's sides as well as the bottom. Pour the batter in a zig-zag motion into the pan. It may sputter and hiss.

Return the pan to the oven and bake for 25 to 30 minutes. Remove from the oven, and serve the cornbread while still warm.

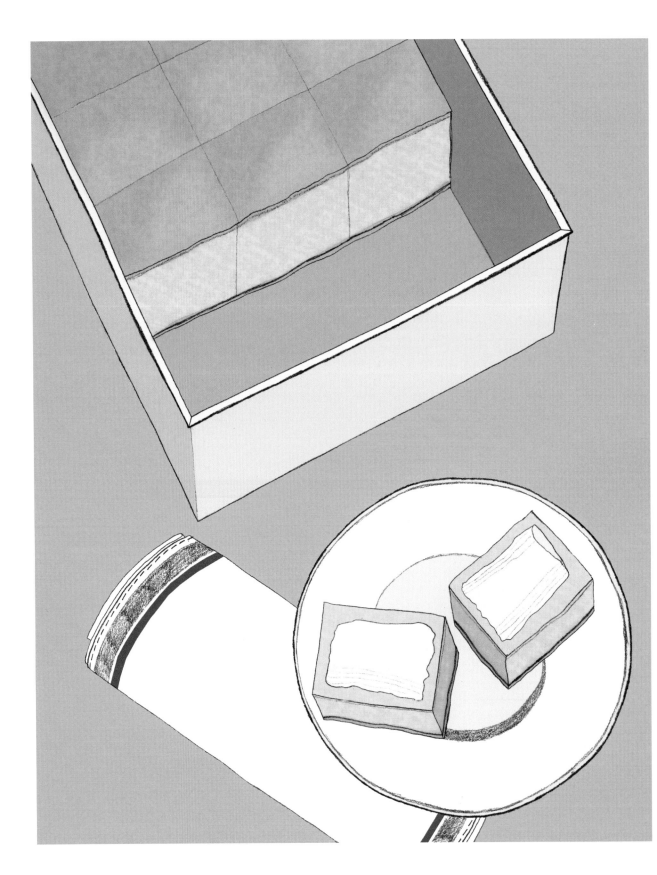

Northern Cornbread

IT COULD BE BECAUSE OF THE LONG, OFTEN HARSH WINTERS, BUT UP NORTH, THEY HAVE ALWAYS baked their cornbread to be soft and rather sweet—the perfect bread to take the chill out of your bones. This cornbread is classic. With a mixture of all-purpose flour and cornmeal, there is a levity to this bread; it's more cake-like than the Southern variety. The sugar, although adding a general sweetness, also elevates the corn flavor. I bake this cornbread in my cast-iron skillet, but it bakes up well in an 8-inch square pan, or even in muffin tins. This bread is great fresh from the oven, but I also love it split, buttered, and then grilled for breakfast the next morning.

Makes 1 9- or 10-inch skillet

2 cups (10 ounces) fine-grained cornmeal

1 cup (5 ounces) all-purpose flour

⅓ cup (2½ ounces) sugar

1 tablespoon baking powder

1 teaspoon kosher salt

2 eggs

2 cups whole milk

4 tablespoons (2 ounces) unsalted butter, melted

Preheat oven to 400°F. Butter a skillet, or lightly coat it with cooking spray. Set aside.

In a medium-size bowl, whisk the cornmeal, flour, sugar, baking powder, and salt together, until free of lumps. Set aside.

In another bowl, whisk the eggs and the milk together.

All at once, pour the wet ingredients into the dry ingredients. Mix until combined, and then add the melted butter, folding it into the batter.

Pour the batter into the prepared skillet, spreading it out if needed. Bake 25 to 30 minutes, or until firm to the touch and slightly cracked on top. If baking in a muffin tin, the muffins will bake for a shorter amount of time, approximately 20 minutes. Remove the cornbread from the oven, and cool for a few minutes on a rack before slicing.

Shaker Cornbread

DURING THE EARLY 1800S, THE SHAKERS, A RELIGIOUS GROUP WHO VALUED PURITY, SIMPLICITY, frugality, and honest work, found corn to be one of the first crops to take root in their burgeoning farming communities. As the years passed, and as other crops began to flourish, the Shakers never forgot the importance of this hardy crop, and they continued to cook and bake with cornmeal.

In the 1953 book, *The Shaker Cook Book: Not by Bread Alone*, author Caroline B. Piercy devotes an entire chapter to the all-important cornmeal. This is an adaptation of a Shaker cornbread from this book. Much like the core values of the Shaker sect, it is simple. Made with light sour cream or whole plain yogurt, this cornbread is unadorned and ultimately sustaining. It uses very little embellishment—and you will find that none is needed. With relatively little else flavoring this bread, the true nature of the cornmeal comes through. The batter is thick due to the sour cream; but it bakes up light and delicious. If ever a food was an example of a philosophy, this cornbread is it.

Makes 1 8-inch square pan

1 cup (5 ounces) fine-grained cornmeal

1 cup (5 ounces) all-purpose flour

1 teaspoon baking soda

1 teaspoon cream of tartar

2 tablespoons sugar

1 teaspoon kosher salt

1 cup (8 ounces) light sour cream
or plain whole milk yogurt

½ cup whole milk

1 egg

1 tablespoon (½ ounce) unsalted butter, melted

Preheat oven to 425°F. Butter an 8-inch square pan, or lightly coat it with cooking spray. Set aside.

In a mixing bowl, whisk the cornmeal, flour, baking soda, cream of tartar, sugar, and salt together until well-combined. Set aside.

In a medium-size bowl, whisk the sour cream or yogurt, milk, and egg together. Add the butter, stirring to combine.

All at once, pour the wet ingredients into the dry ingredients. Mix well; the batter should still have lumps but be thoroughly combined.

Pour the batter into the prepared pan, shaking gently to evenly distribute. Bake for 20 to 25 minutes, or until crusty and golden brown. Remove the cornbread from the oven, and serve while still warm.

Modern Cornbread

SOUTHERN OR NORTHERN, OLD SCHOOL OR NEW, CORNBREAD CONTINUES TO GROW AND ADAPT IN OUR culinary lexicon. This modern interpretation is light in texture because it calls for one extra step—separating the eggs, and whipping the egg whites to frothy peaks. I find this step brings a lightness to this bread that can't be matched. It also uses butter—browned butter—as the fat, making the bread nutty and multi-dimensional. Lastly, whole corn kernels are mixed into the batter, giving the bread a satisfying chewiness. I think this cornbread strikes the perfect balance between sweet and salty, crunchy yet chewy, and it's crumbly enough to satisfy even the most traditional of diners!

Makes 1 8-inch square pan

8 tablespoons (4 ounces) unsalted butter

I cup (5 ounces) fine-grained cornmeal

¼ cup (1 ½ ounces) coarse cornmeal,
such as grits or polenta

I cup (5 ounces) all-purpose flour

I tablespoon baking powder

⅓ cup (2 ¾ ounces) sugar

I ½ teaspoons kosher salt

3 eggs, separated

I cup whole milk

½ cup (2½ ounces) corn kernels,
fresh or frozen

Preheat oven to 350°F. Butter an 8-inch square pan, or lightly coat it with cooking spray. Set aside.

In a medium-size stainless steel or other light-colored saucepan (you'll need to really see the color of the butter as it cooks) over medium heat, melt the butter. Once melted, the butter will begin to foam; as this subsides, continue to cook, swirling the pan, keeping a close eye on its contents. The butter will begin to color and become highly aromatic. Watch it closely. When it turns a light, nut-brown color, immediately take it off the heat.

This should take about 5 minutes. Pour the butter into a separate bowl to ensure that it stops cooking.

In a mixing bowl, whisk both the cornmeals, flour, baking powder, sugar, and salt together until well-combined. Set aside.

In a medium-size bowl, whip the egg whites until frothy and stiff, but not completely dry. Set aside. Mix the browned butter with the milk and egg yolks until combined.

All at once, add the egg yolk mixture to the dry ingredients. Stir with a rubber spatula until thoroughly mixed. Fold the egg whites completely into the batter until no streaks of egg white remain. Lastly, fold in the corn kernels until mixed.

Pour the batter into the prepared pan, spreading it out if needed. Bake 25 to 30 minutes, or until firm to the touch and slightly cracked on top. Remove the cornbread from the oven, and cool for a few minutes on a rack before slicing.

FLATBREADS & FRYBREADS

WE ARE A NATION OF SNACKERS, AND THIS CHAPTER IS TESTAMENT TO that nature. Here you will commune with your rolling pin to make crisp crackers and take comfort with your fryer to cook up golden treats. Unlike many of the other breads in this book, the flatbreads actually get better—drier, crispier, more savory—with each passing day. Some you may be familiar with (or at least with the store-bought version) some of the others may be a new culinary experience. Either way, flour up your rolling pin, and snack away!

Cheese Straws

SITTING ON THE FRONT PORCH WITH A FROSTY GLASS OF SWEET TEA, DABBING THE SWEAT OFF YOUR hairline, the swampy humidity could almost get to you—except you have a pile of salty, piquant cheese straws to munch on as the sun finally begins to set. These straws are *the* cocktail hour snack in the South. Made similarly to pie dough, you simply roll out the cheesy dough and then slice it into manageable lengths. With just enough spice to perk up your palate, these snacks are very addictive, so it's a good thing that one recipe makes around thirty straws. Some Southerners get fancy by twisting the dough before they bake them, but I have always left them in a slightly wobbly straw shape—they get gobbled up so quickly anyway. Make this old-fashioned treat for a mid-afternoon snack or your very own cocktail hour. They are just as tasty when you're living up North as they are when you're south of the Mason-Dixon.

Makes about 30 straws

1½ cups (7½ ounces) all-purpose flour

½ teaspoon dried ground mustard

¼ teaspoon crushed red pepper flakes

¾ teaspoon kosher salt

1½ cups (6 ounces) sharp cheddar cheese, grated

1 teaspoon Worcestershire sauce

6 tablespoons (3 ounces) unsalted butter

7 tablespoons ice water

Preheat oven to 350°F.

In a food processor, pulse the flour, ground mustard, red pepper, and salt together to blend. Add the cheese, and continue pulsing to blend. Add the Worcestershire sauce, butter, and water, and process until the dough comes together to form a ball.

Remove the dough from the food processor, and on a well-floured surface, knead it briefly. The warmth from your hands will slightly melt the cheese and butter, bringing the dough together into a cohesive mass. Lightly flour both the work surface and top of the dough, then roll it out into a rectangle, approximately 14 x 12 inches in diameter, and $1/4$ to $1/8$ inch thick. With a sharp knife or a rotary pizza cutter, slice the dough into strips about $1/3$ inch thick. Place strips on a parchment-lined baking sheet; this may require two baking sheets. The straws will spread very little during baking, so it is fine to bake them close to one another.

Bake for 15 to 18 minutes, or until the straws are barely brown at the tips. Remove them from the oven, let them cool slightly on the pans, then remove them to a cooling rack to cool additionally. Cheese straws can be eaten while still warm and will keep, wrapped, for a few days.

Benne Wafers

A CLOSE FRIEND OF MINE WENT ON A TRIP TO CHARLESTON, SOUTH CAROLINA, AND KNOWING MY penchant for vintage cookbooks, returned home with a copy of *Charleston Receipts* for me. It was a gift that he was sure I would love—and he was correct. This spiral-bound collection is the oldest Junior League—a national volunteer organization for woman—cookbook in print. First printed in 1950, it reads like a history lesson of the American South, with recipes for can-apés, aspics, and casseroles, as well as down home classics—like the benne wafer.

Benne—or sesame seeds—were brought to this country in the seventeenth and eigh-teenth centuries during the slave trade. The crop flourished in the South, and benne seeds were frequently used in baking.

This recipe, adapted from *Charleston Receipts*, is essentially a sesame cracker. The dough is short and flaky, and the wafers are full of roasted sesame, making them savory and nutty all at once. Benne wafers make a wonderful addition to a cheese plate or are delicious all on their own.

Makes approximately 3 dozen

⅓ cup (1½ ounces) sesame seeds

I cup (5 ounces) all-purpose flour

⅛ teaspoon cayenne pepper

½ teaspoon table salt

4 tablespoons (2 ounces) unsalted butter,
chilled and cut into ½-inch dice

I egg yolk, beaten

5 tablespoons ice water

Preheat oven to 350°F. Roast the sesame seeds for 15 to 18 minutes, or until golden brown. Cool completely.

In a medium-size bowl, whisk the flour, cayenne pepper, and salt together. Add the butter, and with your fingers, begin to work the butter into the flour mixture until a coarse meal is obtained. Add the sesame seeds, egg yolk, and water to the mixture, and blend until the mixture begins to form a dough. Knead briefly.

Place the dough on a well-floured work surface. Lightly flour the top of the dough as well, and roll it out to no more than ⅛ inch thick. With a small, 1½ to 2-inch biscuit cutter, cut wafers from the dough. The crackers will spread very little during baking, so it is fine to place them close to each other on a parchment-lined baking sheet.

Bake for 16 to 20 minutes, or until the wafers are lightly browned around the edges. Baking time will be dependent on the size and how thick the wafers are. Remove them from the oven, let them cool slightly on the pan, and then remove to a cooling rack to cool completely. Wafers will continue to firm and crisp as they cool. Store them in an airtight container for up to one week.

TABLE SALT

You'll notice that many of the cracker recipes in this book call for table salt while the bread recipes call for kosher. Table salt is a finer crystal, and with little-to-no rise time, I find that table salt is absorbed into the dough with ease.

Whole Wheat Crackers

AMERICANS LOVE TO SNACK—SO LET'S SNACK RIGHT. IF YOU HAVE NEVER ATTEMPTED BAKING YOUR own crackers, put down whatever you are doing, wander to the kitchen, tie on your apron, and give it a try. You will not be sorry that you did. I might even hazard a guess and say that you will never want to return to the days of store-bought crackers again.

If you have ever looked at the ingredients listed on the back of box of snacks, then you have encountered the list of unpronounceable, multi-syllabic preservatives that they are comprised of. It doesn't have to be that way. At their purest, a cracker is just a handful of delectable ingredients, rolled, cut, and of course, baked.

These wheat crackers are an exercise in balance—salty and sweet, light and hearty—and they taste nutty from the abundance of whole wheat flour. The most difficult part to making crackers is rolling them out. The thinner the dough is rolled, the crisper the cracker will be. This dough is not too sticky, and the gluten structure is not too strong, so rolling the dough is relatively easy. Just make sure your work surface is well-floured; it would be a shame to roll out your dough very thin only to have it stick, making the transfer to the baking sheet impossible.

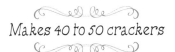

Makes 40 to 50 crackers

1¼ cups (6¼ ounces) whole wheat flour

¾ teaspoon table salt,
plus more for sprinkling

2 tablespoons honey

4 tablespoons (2 ounces) unsalted butter, chilled

5 tablespoons ice water

Preheat oven to 400°F, arranging the racks on the bottom and top thirds of the oven.

In the bowl of a food processor, pulse the flour, table salt, and honey until combined. Add the butter, and continue to pulse until the mixture resembles a coarse meal. With the processor on, add the water. Continue to process until the dough begins to form a ball. This may require a bit more water. If so, add a bit of ice water by the teaspoonful.

Place the dough on a well-floured work surface. Lightly flour the top of the dough as well, and roll it out to no more than ⅛ inch thick. With a cookie cutter or small, 1½-inch biscuit cutter, cut cracker shapes from the dough. Alternately, to make squares, with a sharp knife or a pizza cutter, cut 1½-inch squares from the dough. Place the crackers on two parchment-lined baking sheets. The crackers will spread very little during baking, so it is fine to place them close to each other. With the tines of a fork, prick each cracker several times. Sprinkle additional salt on top, patting the salt lightly into the crackers.

Bake for 8 to 12 minutes, or until lightly browned around the edges, rotating the pans halfway through the baking process. The baking time will be dependent upon how thick the crackers are. Remove them from the oven, let them cool slightly on the pan, and then remove to a cooling rack to cool completely. Crackers will continue to firm and crisp as they cool. Store them in an airtight container for up to one week.

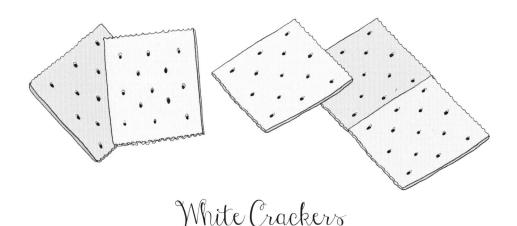

White Crackers

MY MOTHER PUTS A SLICK OF BUTTER ON TOP OF HER CRACKERS BEFORE SHE DUNKS THEM INTO HER soup. I do, too. There is something pleasing about having the cracker sop up the broth while the butter melts into the soup. But one taste of these crisp, satisfying crackers has me rethinking this childhood tradition

Adapted from *The Fanny Farmer Cookbook* the cookbook penned by the late doyenne of American cuisine, Marion Cunningham, this cracker is composed of a handful of ingredients but bakes up into more than the sum of its parts. The dough is easy to work with—the thinner it is rolled out, the crisper your cracker will be. And it bakes into a blistery and snappy cracker. It is simple and very good, spread with butter, or not.

Makes approximately 3 dozen

I cup (5 ounces) all-purpose flour

I teaspoon sugar

½ teaspoon table salt

2 tablespoons (I ounce) unsalted butter, chilled

¼ cup ice water

Preheat oven to 400°F.

In the bowl of a food processor, pulse the flour, sugar, and table salt until combined. Add the butter, and continue to pulse until the mixture resembles a coarse meal. With the food processor on, add the water. Continue to process until the dough begins to form a ball. This may require a bit more water. If so, add a bit of ice water by the teaspoonful.

Place the dough on a well-floured work surface. Lightly flour the top of the dough as well, and roll out to no more than $1/8$ inch thick. With a sharp knife or a pizza cutter, cut $1\frac{1}{2}$-inch squares from the dough. Place the crackers on a parchment-lined baking sheet. The crackers will spread very little during baking, so it is fine to place them close to each other.

Bake for 14 to 17 minutes, or until lightly browned around the edges. The crackers will blister and puff. The baking time will be dependent upon how thick the crackers are. Remove them from the oven, let them cool slightly on the pan, and then remove them to a cooling rack to cool completely. The crackers will continue to firm and to crisp as they cool. Store them in an airtight container for up to one week.

New York Flatbreads

IN THE SUBTERRANEAN DINING CONCOURSE OF GRAND CENTRAL STATION, ACROSS FROM THE CON-gested train platforms, sits the regal Grand Central Oyster Bar. Opened in 1913 and catering to passengers traveling to and from New York, the bar fell into disrepair and was eventually closed in the early 1970s. Refurbished and reopened in 1974, this stunning space, with marble columns and a counter snaking its way through the restaurant, is a true American dining institution.

Being attached to one of the busiest train stations in the United States means that diners are usually in a hurry to grab a bite. As you saddle up to the counter, your place is wiped clean, and a small plate of crackers is set down before you. There are the standard oyster crackers (it is an oyster bar, after all), and next to them is a small stack of rectangular, seeded wheat crackers called New York Flatbreads to nosh on while you peruse the menu. The oyster crack-ers are an expected salty snack, but the flatbread is an addictive standout.

This crisp cracker was created in 1913 by socialite Thelma Eubanks as an alternative to thin Melba toasts. She grew tired of serving caviar on those bland, white toasts! Her flat-breads grew in popularity, Melba toasts were all but forgotten, and a new fad took their place. Coated in seeds, much like an "everything" bagel, this cracker is delightful smeared with soft cheeses, but it has a wholesome crunch that stands up well unadorned, too. For those living more than a train ride away from Grand Central Station, here is a recipe to compete with the New York Flatbread at the Oyster Bar. Nutty from whole wheat flour, with just the right amount of crunch, these hearty crackers make a wonderful addition to your hors d'oeuvres platter, caviar or not!

Makes 40 to 50 flatbreads

1 cup (5 ounces) all-purpose flour

¾ cup (3¾ ounces) whole wheat flour

¾ teaspoon baking powder

1 teaspoon kosher salt

1 teaspoon sugar

¼ cup vegetable or canola oil

1 teaspoon distilled white vinegar

TOPPING:

1 tablespoon sesame seeds

1½ teaspoons poppy seeds

1½ teaspoons dehydrated minced onion

Preheat oven to 425°F, arranging the racks on the bottom and top thirds of the oven.

In a medium-size bowl, whisk the flours, baking powder, salt, and sugar together until well-combined and free of lumps. Set aside. In another bowl, combine ½ cup water with the oil and vinegar. Pour the wet ingredients into the dry ingredients, and mix. The mixture may require some kneading to form a dough.

Divide the dough in half. Cover one portion of it with plastic wrap to avoid drying the dough out. On a well-floured surface, roll out the other portion of dough in a circular shape, as thinly as possible, about ⅛ inch thick. With a sharp knife or a rotary pizza cutter, make slices 1½ to 2 inches thick across the dough. It is fine if the dough is jagged and irregular along the perimeter. Cut each strip into 4-inch pieces. Place the pieces on a baking sheet. The flatbreads will spread very little during baking, so it is fine to place them close to each other. Repeat the process with the second portion of dough, placing the flatbreads on another baking sheet.

In a small bowl, mix the sesame seeds, poppy seeds, and onion. Brush the dough with water, and then sprinkle the topping evenly amongst the two baking sheets. With your hand, gently press the topping into the surface of the cracker.

Bake for 14 to 17 minutes, rotating the baking sheets once, halfway through the baking process. Remove them from the oven, and let the crackers cool on a rack. The crackers should be lightly browned at the edges, and they will crisp more upon cooling.

Graham Biscuits

WHILE SYLVESTER GRAHAM, THE NINETEENTH CENTURY PREACHER AND HEALTH-NUT, MAY HAVE BEEN the originator of the graham biscuit, it wasn't until the National Biscuit Company, known today as Nabisco, created their Honey Maid brand of graham biscuits and changed the name to *graham crackers* that these became a staple in American's snack food diet. Originally made completely with graham flour, entirely unsweetened, and relatively bland, the graham cracker of yore was almost unrecognizable from what it is today. Now these crackers are almost like cookies, used in pie shells and as a cradle for a gooey s'more.

If you like a store-bought graham cracker, let me assure you, you will love a homemade graham biscuit. They are reminiscent of a graham cracker, but they are darker, richer, oatier. Assembled in moments in a food processor, refrigerated briefly, and then rolled-out and baked, these biscuits are a lovely mid-afternoon snack, but they are wonderful for breakfast as well. (I spread them with peanut butter.) They are crisp, like a cracker, and will stay fresh for about a week in an airtight container. But I don't think they will last that long!

Makes about 45 2-inch square biscuits

¾ cup (3¾ ounces) all-purpose flour

1½ cups (7½ ounces) graham flour

½ cup (3 ounces) brown sugar, packed

1 teaspoon baking powder

½ teaspoon baking soda

½ teaspoon kosher salt

8 tablespoons (4 ounces) unsalted butter, cold, cut into ½-inch pieces

2 tablespoons honey

2 tablespoons molasses

½ cup ice water

In the bowl of a food processor, pulse both of the flours, the brown sugar, baking powder, baking soda, and salt until combined. Add the butter, and continue to pulse until the mixture resembles a coarse meal. Add the honey, molasses, and water, and process until the dough comes together to form a ball.

Place the dough on a piece of plastic wrap. Form it into a circle, and flatten the dough to ½ inch thick. Refrigerate until firm, about 1 hour.

Preheat the oven to 350°F, arranging the racks on the bottom and top thirds of the oven.

Place the dough on a well-floured work surface. Lightly flour the top of the dough as well, and roll out to approximately ⅛ inch. With a sharp knife or a rotary pizza cutter, make slices about 2 inches in diameter. Make additional slices to create biscuits, about 2 inches square. Place the biscuits on two parchment-lined baking sheets. The biscuits will spread very little during baking, so it is fine to place them close to each other. With the tines of a fork, prick each biscuit several times.

Bake for 14 to 18 minutes, or until lightly browned at the edges, rotating the pans once during the baking process. Remove them from the oven, let them cool slightly on the pans, then remove them to a cooling rack to cool completely. Biscuits will firm and crisp as they cool. Store them in an airtight container for up to one week.

Sopaipillas

IF YOU'RE FAMILIAR WITH THE FOOD OF THE AMERICAN SOUTHWEST, THEN YOU HAVE PROBABLY HAVE seen baskets of these puffed fry breads sitting on dining tables at restaurants or in homes throughout New Mexico. But peculiarly, these delicious pillows have not really caught on throughout the rest of the country. Thought to have originated in Albuquerque, New Mexico some 200 years ago, the name derives from the word Spanish word *sopaipa*, meaning honey cake. Akin to Mexican fry breads, this non-yeasted, simply flavored bread is definitely not a donut, but it's not really a fritter either—although it is fried in the same fashion. Rolled into a flat disk and then cut into wedges, the dough is fried in hot oil, so it blisters and puffs. Due to a bit of baking powder in the mix, sopaipillas create a cavern for mostly sweet fillings. Although served with chili sauce as well, typically these beauties are eaten straight from the fryer and served with sticky honey. Drizzled inside, the honey soaks into the bread, making a delectable coating.

Sopaipillas are a quick and decadent treat. Unlike a raised doughnut or even a muffin, they can be mixed up and fried in less than an hour, making a unique and delightful Sunday morning meal. I prefer my sopaipillas on the smaller side, so this recipe makes twelve. If you decide that you like a larger pillow, simply roll out two rounds of dough, and make eight slightly larger sopaipillas.

Makes 12 sopaipillas

2 cups (10 ounces) all-purpose flour

1 teaspoon baking powder

1 teaspoon sugar

1 teaspoon kosher salt

2 tablespoons (about ½ ounce) vegetable shortening,
cut into ½-inch pieces

¼ cup whole milk

½ cup warm water (100° to 115°F)

Oil for frying (vegetable, canola, or other flavorless oil)

In a medium-size bowl, whisk the flour, baking powder, sugar, and salt together until thoroughly mixed. With your fingertips, work the vegetable shortening into the flour mixture until coarse crumbs are formed. Add the milk and water, and stir with a wooden spoon until a sticky dough is formed.

Empty the dough onto a clean work surface, and knead until smooth, about 2 minutes. Knead the dough into a ball, and cover it with a moist tea towel. Let the dough rest for approximately 30 minutes.

Divide the dough into 3 equal portions. Form one portion of dough into a circle. Again, on a clean surface (the dough will have rested and should not be too sticky), roll the dough out into a circle, approximately 10 inches in diameter, and $\frac{1}{4}$ to $\frac{1}{8}$ inch thick. Cut the circle into four wedges. Repeat with other portions of dough, in order to get 12 pieces total.

In a Dutch oven or other deep pan, pour oil approximately 2 inches deep. Heat to 375° to 400°F. Carefully add 3 wedges of dough. The dough will sink, but it will soon rise and begin to puff. Fry until golden brown on one side, about 30 seconds to 1 minute. With a slotted spoon, flip the sopaipillas over, and continue to fry until golden brown, another 30 seconds or so. Remove them from the hot oil, and drain on paper towels. Make sure to reheat the oil to 375° to 400°F before frying the next batches. It is important that the oil remain hot so the sopaipillas do not absorb much oil during frying.

Serve the sopaipillas immediately with honey.

DRIED BREAD

I AM SURE THAT YOU HAVE HEARD THE PHRASE: *WASTE NOT, WANT NOT.* IF you take these words to heart, then this is the chapter for you!

The day that you bake bread, it may require all of your restraint not to spread each freshly baked slice with butter and consume the entire loaf. The second day the novelty of the bread may have worn some—but it still makes great toast in the morning, providing delicious nourishment. By day three, the sparkle may have tarnished even more. This is the day to turn to the recipes in this chapter. A dry loaf of bread just needs a bit of revitalizing: a simmer in stock, a douse of custard, or a dunk in egg. Who knows, you may find some of these recipes so delicious that you're leaving loaves of bread out to dry especially for them.

Savory Bread Pudding with Mushrooms and Kale

WE ALL KNOW ABOUT SWEET BREAD PUDDING, BUT WHAT ABOUT *SAVORY* BREAD PUDDING— overflowing with vegetables, eggy and rich, warm and satisfying. This pudding is made with broth rather than milk, so it is looser, but it is the broth that imparts a wonderful depth of flavor. Perfect as a vegetarian entrée or a side dish to a meal of roast chicken, this pudding is extremely versatile. Upon baking, the top gets crisp and crackly, while the bottom slumps, getting soft and sumptuous. In this recipe, I suggest making the pudding with woodsy, meaty mushrooms and gently sautéed kale, but feel free to substitute as the seasons allows—cherry tomatoes and corn, roasted butternut squash and spinach—the combinations abound. This savory bread pudding is perfect with any of the hardier breads in the sourdough chapter (pages 63–81).

Serves 4 as an entrée, 6 as a side dish

3 tablespoons (1½ ounces) unsalted butter, divided

2 tablespoons olive oil

2 yellow onions, thinly sliced

Salt and pepper, to taste

2 cups (4 ounces) shitake or cremini mushrooms, sliced

1 bunch (4 loosely packed cups) kale, cleaned, stemmed, and torn into bite-sized pieces

2 cups chicken or vegetable broth, divided

6 cups (8 ounces) sourdough bread, cut into 1-inch cubes

2 teaspoons fresh thyme, coarsely chopped

1 cup (4 ounces) Gruyere cheese, grated

3 eggs

In a large skillet over medium-high heat, melt 2 tablespoons of butter in the olive oil. Add the onion, season with salt and pepper, and cook for 10 to 15 minutes, or until the onions are beginning to brown and have reduced in volume by half. Add the mushrooms. Stir well, and then leave for a moment, allowing the mushrooms to exude their moisture and begin to brown, about 2 minutes. Toss in the kale, stirring to coat with any moisture left in the pan. Add ½ cup of broth and continue to cook until the kale wilts and the broth cooks out of the vegetable mixture, about 2 minutes. Taste for seasoning, and if necessary, add additional salt and pepper.

Preheat the oven to 375°F. Grease an 8-inch square or 2-quart baking dish with remaining butter.

In a large mixing bowl, toss the vegetables with the dried bread. Add the thyme and cheese, tossing well to combine. Pour the bread mixture into the baking dish, and if necessary, evenly distribute the vegetables amongst the bread cubes.

In a medium-size bowl, beat the remainder of the broth and the eggs together. Season the mixture with salt and pepper. Pour the egg mixture over the bread and vegetables, and leave to set for 10 minutes, letting the mixture soften and meld together.

Bake for 30 to 35 minutes. The pudding should be brown and crusty on top, and the custard set. Enjoy while hot.

Tomato-Cornbread Soup

PAPPA AL POMODORO, OR TOMATO-BREAD SOUP, IS THE MINGLING OF VINE-RIPENED TOMATOES, DRIED bread, and lots of fresh basil—it is delicious simplicity at its finest. This Italian dish is also a frugal way to use up each and every last crust of bread. I was wondering what the American equivalent of this recipe would be. What would our the match for a ubiquitous, rustic Italian loaf be? Then it came to me, down-home cornbread, a bread that has been gracing American tables for centuries.

My take on the soup uses canned tomatoes (so you can make this recipe during any season), and the sturdier, woodsy herb, rosemary, for earthiness. When the cornbread meets the simmering tomatoes, it relaxes into a soft, polenta-like consistency. The soup is rib-sticking with a gentle grittiness from the cornmeal. For a quick weeknight meal, just toss a salad alongside, and dinner is ready.

Serves 4

I 28-ounce can whole tomatoes

2 tablespoons olive oil

I tablespoon (½ ounce) unsalted butter

I medium yellow onion, diced

Salt and pepper, to taste

I garlic clove, minced

I teaspoon fresh rosemary, minced

I cup chicken stock or water

2 cups dried cornbread, cut into I-inch cubes

In a medium-size bowl, crush the whole tomatoes with their juice by hand, making sure there are no large pieces left. Set aside.

In a large saucepan or Dutch oven, over medium heat, melt the olive oil and the butter. Add the onion, season with salt and pepper, and continue to cook until the onion becomes translucent, about 3 to 5 minutes. Add the garlic and rosemary, and continue to sauté until fragrant, about 1 minute.

Add the tomatoes and the stock, and bring to a boil. Reduce heat to a simmer, cover, and cook for 15 minutes.

Add the cornbread, breaking up pieces with a spoon and letting them dissolve into the soup. Continue to simmer for 5 to 10 minutes. Taste for seasoning, adding additional salt and pepper if needed. With the addition of the cornbread, the soup should be thick and almost creamy.

Bread Soup with Winter Vegetables

IT'S A NO-BRAINER THAT SOUP IS FITTING FOR A WINTERTIME MEAL. A POT FULL OF HEARTY VEGETA-bles simmering on the stove is a comforting and nourishing meal. As the bonus, your kitchen will smell terrific—it's as if you're calling everyone to dinner just by turning on the stove. Here is another take on bread soup, but this recipe utilizes those ruddy winter vegetables that are so often cellared for the season. A mix of carrots, parsnips, cauliflower, butternut squash—whatever you have on hand—are roasted, concentrating their flavor. Then the vegetables are added to the porridge of broth and bread cubes, and dinner is served.

Use a savory bread in this recipe; most of the sourdough breads (pages 63–75) make satisfying bread soup.

Serves 4

6 cups mixed winter vegetables (carrots, parsnips, cauliflower, etc.), cut into ½-inch dice

2 tablespoons olive oil, divided

Salt and pepper, to taste

1 medium yellow onion, diced

2 garlic cloves, sliced thinly

4 cups chicken or vegetable broth

4 cups (5 ounces) dried bread, cut into 1-inch cubes

2 tablespoons flat-leaf parsley, roughly chopped

Preheat oven to 425°F.

On a baking sheet, toss the vegetables in 1 tablespoon of olive oil, and season with salt and pepper. Roast for 35 to 40 minutes, or until the vegetables are caramelized and softened.

Meanwhile, in a large saucepan or Dutch oven, heat the remaining olive oil over medium heat. When shimmering, add the onion and sauté until translucent, about 3 to 5 minutes. Add the garlic, and continue to cook until fragrant, about 1 minute. Pour in the broth, and bring to a simmer.

Turn the heat down to low, and add the bread. Allow the mixture to cook at a gentle simmer for approximately 10 minutes. The bread will fully absorb the liquid, soften, and eventually fall apart. Depending on the bread that you use, this may require some assistance. With a wooden spoon, crush the bread cubes against the side of the pot, or use a potato masher. The soup should have the consistency of a loose porridge or oatmeal. More liquid can be added if the soup is becoming too thick. Add up to 2 cups of water if needed.

Add the roasted vegetables and the parsley, stirring well. Heat through. Taste for seasoning, and then serve immediately.

PARMESAN CHEESE

Grated on a weeknight pasta, or shaved into a salad, this ingredient has become ubiquitous in American kitchens; but what do you do with Parmesan rinds when you've scraped the last bit of cheese? I freeze them. The rind has a tremendous amount of briny, umami flavor, which is wonderful in soups. Simply store the rind in the freezer until you make your next pot. No need even to bring the rind to room temperature; just drop it in the soup you are preparing. It will impart a ton of flavor while the soup is simmering away; just remove it before serving. The rind will have melted some, but it should still be intact. This rind can add a superb layer of flavor to this Bread Soup.

Wild Rice Bread Stuffing

I NEVER LET MY BREAD SPOIL OR GO TO WASTE. SO THAT MEANS AT MY HOUSE, WE EAT A LOT OF stuffing—even when it's not Thanksgiving. Stuffing pairs well with so many entrées—from roasts of all kind to juicy, seared steaks—and is warm, comforting, and delicious.

I make stuffing from all kinds of savory bread in this book, from sourdough to whole wheat loaves, but one of my favorites is the Wild Rice Bread (page 32). The bread is great, but the stuffing, with its soft bread and nutty wild rice, makes a superlative winter side dish. It's like having the best of both worlds—a rice stuffing and a traditional bread stuffing, too! Just make sure your bread is really stale; that way, it will absorb all of the flavors permeating the recipe. When I make this stuffing, I slice the bread and then lay it out overnight. The next morning the bread is perfectly stale and ready to be torn into pieces.

Serves 6

2 tablespoons (1 ounce) unsalted butter, divided

2 tablespoons olive oil

6 cremini mushroom (4 ounces), sliced

3 celery stalks, cut into ½-inch dice

1 large yellow onion, diced

Salt and pepper, to taste

6 cups stale Wild Rice Bread (page 32),
torn into ½-inch pieces

2 eggs, beaten

1½ cups chicken or vegetable broth

2 teaspoons dried ground sage

Preheat oven to 375°F.

Grease an 8-inch square or 1½- to 2-quart round baking dish with 1 tablespoon of butter. Set aside.

In a large skillet, over medium heat, melt the remaining tablespoon of butter in the olive oil. When the foam subsides, add the mushroom, celery, and onion, and toss them in the fat. Leave the vegetables until they start to exude their moisture and begin to turn brown. Season with salt and pepper, and continue to sauté until the vegetables have reduced by half and are golden brown, about 7 to 10 minutes. Remove from heat.

In a large bowl, toss the bread, eggs, broth, and sage until combined. Add the vegetables, and continue to mix until well-combined. Pour the stuffing mixture into the prepared baking dish, pressing the mixture down evenly.

Bake for 35 to 40 minutes, or until the top of the stuffing is crisp and golden brown.

Tomato Bread Salad

IN ITALY, THIS TIME-HONORED DISH USING DRIED CRUSTS OF BREAD PRACTICALLY SCREAMS SUMMER.
My recipe observes the classic details, but has one added, delectable step—roasting some
of the tomatoes. I love to make this salad in the late summer, when there is a confluence of
tomatoes (both the heavy beefsteak variety and the diminutive cherry tomatoes) and loads
of fresh basil—and when the weather has cooled just a bit so I can actually bear to flip on
the oven. Using both chopped fresh tomatoes and roasted cherry tomatoes gives this salad
an added hit of tomato flavor. By roasting the cherry tomatoes until they blister and pop, the
flavor is concentrated, and the juice exuded is sweet yet savory. Fresh tomatoes are bright
and grassy, providing a juiciness to mingle with the dried bread.

The rest of the salad couldn't be simpler. Bread, basil, tomatoes—how complicated
can that be? I suggest using a coarse, rustic bread, like most of the sourdough breads
(pages 63–75). This salad is perfect on its own as a vegetarian lunch, or great as a dinner with
a piece of fish.

Serves 6

I pint (2½ cups) cherry tomatoes, cleaned, and stemmed

I tablespoon plus ¼ cup olive oil, divided

Salt and pepper, to taste

3 tablespoons red wine vinegar or sherry vinegar

I to 1¼ pounds (about 3 large) beefsteak or heirloom tomatoes,
cleaned and cut into a 1-inch dice

¼ red onion, thinly sliced

4 cups (5 ounces) dried bread, cut into 1-inch cubes

½ cup loosely packed basil, torn or chiffonaded

Preheat oven to 350°F.

In a small baking dish, toss the cherry tomatoes in 1 tablespoon of the olive oil, and
season well with salt and pepper.

Bake for 45 to 50 minutes, or until wilted and blistered. The tomatoes should have
given off a substantial amount of juice. Transfer the tomatoes and the juice to a separate
dish, and cool to room temperature. This step can be completed a few days ahead of time.

Simply refrigerate the tomatoes and juices, and then bring them back to room temperature before proceeding with the rest of the recipe.

In a small bowl, whisk together the vinegar and the remaining ¼ cup of olive oil. Season well with salt and pepper.

In a large bowl, gently toss the roasted tomatoes, fresh tomatoes, and red onion together. Pour the vinaigrette over the mixture, season again with salt, and allow it to sit for approximately 15 minutes. With the addition of salt, the tomatoes will continue to exude liquid.

Gently toss in the bread cubes, mixing well to coat the bread in the tomato liquid. Let sit for 15 to 30 minutes. The bread will soften substantially and take on the tomato flavor.

Sprinkle on the basil, toss gently, and serve immediately.

Apple Brown Betty

WHILE NOT QUITE A COBBLER, NOR A CRUMBLE, AND DEFINITELY NOT A CRISP, THIS IS DEFINITELY AN old-fashioned dessert to rival even those classics. So why the name, and just who was Betty? When we first see the appearance of this dessert during the mid-nineteenth century, dishes were often named for the cooks who originated them. Most likely, we have a cook named Betty to thank for mixing sliced apples, sugar, cinnamon, and bread cubes and making this delicious dessert. This is not the type of sweet with a billowy meringue or miles of sky-high frosting; it is warming, comforting, and not too sweet—the perfect dessert to eat on a week-night, after a rib-sticking meal. This dessert takes advantage of dried and buttered sandwich bread cubes. Any one of the sandwich loaves—the Basic White Loaf (page 26), the Buttermilk Bread (page 30), the Whole Wheat Bread (page 31), Pullman loaf (page 60), or even Challah (page 47)—are super when making Apple Brown Betty.

Serves 6

1 tablespoon (½ ounce) unsalted butter, at room temperature

FOR THE BREAD CUBES:

3 cups dried bread cubes, crusts cut off, cut into ¼- to ½-inch cubes

¼ cup (1¾ ounces) sugar

½ teaspoon ground cinnamon

4 tablespoons (2 ounces) unsalted butter, melted

FOR THE APPLES:

5 medium Granny Smith or Pippin apples (about 2 pounds),
peeled, cored, and cut into ¼-inch slices

Zest and juice of 1 medium lemon

½ cup (3 ounces) brown sugar, packed

½ teaspoon cinnamon

¼ teaspoon nutmeg, freshly ground, if possible

¼ teaspoon kosher salt

4 tablespoons (2 ounces) unsalted butter, melted

Preheat oven to 325°F. Grease an 8-inch square baking pan with the butter, and set aside.

In a medium-size bowl, toss the bread cubes with the sugar and cinnamon. Pour in the melted butter, and toss the cubes well to coat them in the butter and to combine them with the sugar and cinnamon. Set aside.

In a large bowl, toss the apples with the lemon zest and juice, brown sugar, cinnamon, nutmeg, and salt. Pour in the melted butter, and toss well to combine. Set aside.

Sprinkle approximately 1 cup of the bread cubes in the bottom of the prepared pan. Pour the apple mixture on top of the cubes, spreading the apples out evenly. Sprinkle the remainder of the bread cubes on top of the apples, patting them gently into the surface of the apples.

Cover the pan with foil, and bake for 40 minutes. Remove the foil, and continue baking for 15 minutes. Remove the pan from the oven; the bread cubes should be toasted and slightly brown, and the Brown Betty will have cooked down some. Enjoy while still warm, or cool to room temperature. This dessert can be served with a scoop of vanilla ice cream or drizzled with cream.

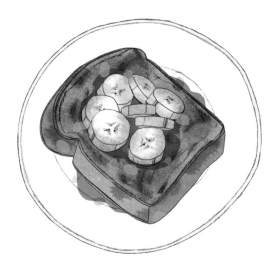

Cornflake-Encrusted French Toast with Sautéed Bananas

CHALLAH FRENCH TOAST HAS BECOME AN AMERICAN DINER CLASSIC, BUT WHAT ABOUT ENCRUSTING that French toast in another breakfast standard—cornflakes? Less-than-fresh challah is the perfect medium with which to make French toast. The dry bread absorbs some of the eggy mixture, making the French toast custardy and luscious, and dredging the toast in crushed cornflakes makes it crisp and crunchy.

I top this French toast goodness with some sliced and sautéed bananas. Caramelized slightly in a pan, then doused with pure maple syrup, the bananas wilt ever so slightly, making an elegant topping to a revamped dish.

Makes 6 slices of French toast

2 cups crushed cornflakes

4 eggs

½ cup whole milk

½ teaspoon orange zest

1 teaspoon vanilla extract

2 tablespoons sugar

Pinch of kosher salt

6 slices Challah (page 47), ¾-inch thick

2 tablespoons (1 ounce) unsalted butter, divided

2 tablespoons vegetable oil, divided

FOR THE BANANAS:

1 tablespoon (½ ounce) unsalted butter

2 firm bananas, sliced into ½-inch pieces

Large pinch of salt

3 tablespoons pure maple syrup,
plus more for serving

Preheat oven to 200°F.

Put the cornflake crumbs in a shallow dish; set aside.

In another shallow dish or 8-inch square baking pan, beat the eggs, milk, orange zest, vanilla, sugar, and salt together, until they're thoroughly mixed. Working with 2 slices of challah at a time, dip the bread into the egg mixture, allowing it to soak for approximately 10 seconds a side. Then coat each slice in the cornflakes, pressing the crumbs into the challah. Set the prepared challah slices on a cutting board or wax paper-lined tray. Repeat with the rest of the bread slices.

In a large, 10-inch skillet over medium heat, melt 1 tablespoon of butter with 1 table-spoon of oil. When the foam subsides and the fats are slightly shimmering, add half of the prepared challah slices, and cook until golden brown, 4 minutes total. Remove the French toast to an ovenproof plate, and put it in the oven to remain warm. Melt the additional butter and oil, and continue to cook the remainder of the French toast until golden brown. The French toast can remain in the warm oven as you prepare the bananas.

In another large skillet, over medium heat, melt the butter. When the foam subsides, add the bananas. Cook them on one side, until they're beginning to caramelize, and then flip them over. Sprinkle liberally with the salt, and continue to cook until they are caramelized on both sides. Pour in the maple syrup. Reduce for about 1 minute, then remove from heat.

Serve the French toast with the sautéed bananas on top and more maple syrup.

Bread and Butter Pudding with Strawberry Sauce

EVERYONE NEEDS A GO-TO DESSERT, ONE THAT IS RELATIVELY SIMPLE, TRUSTWORTHY, AND ABOVE ALL, delectable. This bread pudding is just one of those desserts. Made in the traditional English fashion, this bread pudding is not made with torn pieces of bread, but rather, the stale bread is sliced sandwich-style, buttered, then cut in half, and finally laid in an overlapping fashion in the baking dish. I have augmented the pudding by layering in chopped chocolate. The chocolate melts, creating a bit of decadence to what could have been a rather austere dessert. Accompanying the recipe for this bread pudding is a warm strawberry sauce. Essentially it is a fruit compote, but one that brightens this baked dessert. If it's not strawberry season, feel free to use frozen fruit, or skip the sauce altogether and serve the pudding with whipped cream or *crème fraîche*.

What is lovely about this bread pudding—besides the taste—is its versatility. It can be made with any of the soft white loaves, such as Challah (page 47), Pullman (page 60), or the Basic White Loaf (page 26).

Serves 6 to 8

STRAWBERRY SAUCE:

1 pint (approximately 10 ounces) strawberries,
cleaned and cut into quarters or halves

Zest and juice of 1 medium lemon

2 tablespoons to ¼ cup (1¾ ounces) sugar, depending
on the sweetness of the berries

1 tablespoon vanilla extract

Pinch of salt

BREAD PUDDING.

5 tablespoons (2½ ounces) unsalted butter,
softened to room temperature, divided

3 eggs

1½ cups whole milk

½ cup heavy cream

½ cup (3½ ounces) sugar

1 teaspoon vanilla extract

¼ teaspoon salt

6 to 8 pieces day-old white bread, cut into ½-inch slices

3 ounces semisweet or bittersweet chocolate, chopped

1 tablespoon sanding or turbinado sugar

To make the sauce, in a medium-size saucepan, add the strawberries, lemon zest and juice, sugar, vanilla, and salt. Bring to a boil, and then reduce the heat to a simmer. Cook for 10 to 15 minutes, or until the berries wilt and soften and exude their juices. Taste for sweetness, adding additional sugar if necessary. The sauce should be shiny and slightly thickened. Set aside.

The sauce can also be made a day ahead of time and stored in the refrigerator. Simply bring it back to room temperature, or reheat it on the stove before using.

To make the pudding, grease an 8-inch square or 1½- to 2-quart round baking dish with 1 tablespoon of butter. Set aside.

In a medium-sized bowl, whisk the eggs until frothy. Add the milk, cream, sugar, vanilla, and salt. Continue to whisk until blended; set aside.

With the remaining 4 tablespoons of butter, generously butter one side of each slice of bread. Cut the buttered slices diagonally in half.

Preheat oven to 350°F.

Layer half of the slices of bread, buttered side up, in the baking dish. The bread should slightly overlap. Sprinkle approximately half of the chocolate over the bread. Pour half of the custard mixture over the bread mixture, pressing down the bread to submerge it in the custard. Layer the final slices of bread over the pudding, sprinkle with the rest of the chocolate, and finally pour on the rest of the custard mixture. Press all of the bread slices down to moisten the bread in the custard. Let the pudding sit for 15 minutes to absorb the custard mixture.

Sprinkle the turbinado or sanding sugar over the pudding. Bake for 40 to 45 minutes, or until it's golden brown and the pudding is set. The pudding will puff substantially, but it will settle upon cooling. The bread pudding can be enjoyed while still warm, or cooled to room temperature. It can also be sliced as you would a cake, or spooned out into dishes. Serve with the strawberry sauce both on top and on the side.

Monkey Bread Pudding

MOST OF THE RECIPES IN THIS BOOK ARE FOR DISCRETE LOAVES OF BREAD, HANDHELD ROLLS, OR manageable sweet treats—all of which can be gobbled up by a relatively small group of people. But there are certain recipes, like the Monkey Bread (page 120), that were too delectable to be left out, and whose size may be a little overwhelming for a small party of diners. There is only one thing to do in that situation: Make the Monkey Bread anyway (you won't be sorry that you did), and then make Monkey Bread *Pudding*.

Monkey Bread is one of those breads that is practically dessert already, so taking it one step further by mixing it with a creamy custard and making a pudding out of it is logically delicious. If you don't feel like making bread pudding the very next day you have baked the bread, the leftovers are easily wrapped in plastic and put in the freezer until the dessert bug bites. Simply defrost the leftover Monkey Bread at room temperature, and then proceed with the recipe as follows. The pudding will smell unbelievable while it's baking and is wonderful served still warm, with a dollop of unsweetened whipped cream.

Makes 1 8-inch square pan

3 eggs

¼ cup (1¾ ounces) sugar

¼ cup (1½ ounces) brown sugar, packed

¼ cup maple syrup

½ teaspoon kosher salt

2 cups whole milk

2 teaspoons vanilla

5 tablespoons (2 ½ ounces) unsalted butter,
melted, divided

6 cups cubed Monkey Bread (page 120),
approximately ⅓ of a whole Monkey Bread

¼ cup (1¼ ounces) raisins (optional)

In a medium-size bowl, whisk the eggs, both the sugars, the maple syrup, and the salt together, until well combined. Add the milk, vanilla, and 4 tablespoons of butter, and continue to whisk until combined.

In a large bowl, toss the bread cubes and the raisins, if using. Pour the egg mixture over the bread, mixing to allow all of the bread to be immersed in the custard. Leave the pudding to set for 15 minutes.

Preheat the oven to 350°F. Grease an 8-inch square pan with remaining butter, and set aside.

After 15 minutes have passed, stir the pudding mixture once more to make sure that bread has soaked in the custard mixture. Pour it into the prepared pan, spreading the bread evenly, if needed. Bake for 40 to 45 minutes, or until the pudding has puffed and is golden brown and the custard has set. Remove it from the oven, and cool slightly. The pudding may be served while still warm.

ACKNOWLEDGMENTS

THANK YOU: JENNIFER KASIUS, LINDSEY SPINKS, FRANCES SOO PING CHOW, and Alia Habib. As always, I am so grateful to the family and friends who came along with me on the recipe development, the testing, and the writing—always with eager bellies. Brian Kane, what can I say—you are my biggest supporter and my most eager taste-tester, I love you. Karen Handler, Jennifer Sahadi—thank you for letting me bend your ears. And finally, Ian Quinn, Juan Romero, Michael Thompson, and others who have broken bread with me, I cannot say it enough, thank you.

BIBLIOGRAPHY

Beard, James. 1973. *Beard on Bread.* New York: Knopf.

Clayton, Bernard, and Donnie Cameron. 2003. *Bernard Clayton's New Complete Book of Breads.* New York: Simon & Schuster.

Corbitt, Helen. 1957. *Helen Corbitt's Cookbook.* Houghton Mifflin.

Crump, Nancy Carter. 2008. *Hearthside Cooking: Early American Southern Cuisine Updated for Today's Hearth & Cookstove.* Chapel Hill, NC: University of North Carolina Press.

Cunningham, Marion, and Fannie Merritt Farmer. 1990. *The Fannie Farmer Cookbook.* New York: Knopf.

Dooley, Beth, and Lucia Watson. 1994. *Savoring the Seasons of the Northern Heartland.* New York: Knopf.

Farmer, Fannie Merritt. 1997. *Original 1896 Boston Cooking-School Cookbook.* Mineola, NY: Dover Publications.

Gibson, Charles H. 1894. *Mrs. Charles H. Gibson's Maryland and Virginia Cook Book.* Baltimore, MD: J. Murphy.

Good, Phyllis Pellman, and Rachel T. Pellman. 1984. *From Amish and Mennonite Kitchens.* Intercourse, PA: Good Books.

Gubser, Mary. 1985. *America's Bread Book: 300 Authentic Recipes for America's Favorite Homemade Breads Collected on a 65,000-Mile Journey through the Fifty United States.* New York: Morrow.

Hamelman, Jeffrey. 2004. *Bread: A Baker's Book of Techniques and Recipes.* Hoboken, NJ: John Wiley.

Hanley, Catherine. 1987. *Blue Ribbon Winners: America's Best State Fair Recipes.* Tucson, AZ: HP Books.

Hewitt, Jean. 1972. *The New York Times Heritage Cook Book.* New York: Putnam.

Junior League of Charleston (S.C.), Mary Vereen Huguenin, and Anne Montague Stoney. 2009. *Charleston Receipts.* Charleston, S.C.: Junior League of Charleston.

King Arthur Flour (Firm). 2003. *The King Arthur Flour Baker's Companion: The All-Purpose Baking Cookbook.* Woodstock, VT: Countryman Press.

Lincoln, Mary J. 2013. *The Peerless Cook Book.* 1922. Charleston, SC: Nabu Press.

Malgieri, Nick. 1995. *How to Bake.* New York: William Morrow.

Nichols, Nell Beaubien. 1969. *Homemade Bread.* Garden City, NY: Doubleday.

Piercy, Caroline B. 1953. *The Shaker Cook Book; Not by Bread Alone.* New York: Crown Publishers.

Seranne, Ann. 1967. *America Cooks; The General Federation of Women's Clubs Cookbook.* New York: Putnam.

Standard, Stella. 1970. *Our Daily Bread; 366 Recipes for Wonderful Breads.* New York: Funk & Wagnalls.

Vaughan, Beatrice. 1971. *The Ladies Aid Cookbook.* Brattleboro, VT: Stephen Greene Press.

Virginia Federation of Home Demonstration Clubs. 1958. *Recipes from Old Virginia.* Richmond, V A: Dietz Press.

INDEX